NaturesScope

Unlocking Our Natural Empathy and Creativity.

An inspiring new way of relating to our natural

origins and one another through 'natural inclusion'

Few thinkers are keen to find ways of conversing across conceptual and spatial boundaries. The implications for ethics, human knowledge and human organisation are vital for this generation and the next. Alan is one of the thinkers who is inclusive. He understands that we co-shape one another's thinking, just as we are co-shaped by the landscape.

Dr Janet McIntyre

Associate Professor, Flinders Institute of Public Policy and Management, Adelaide

Rayner's idea of natural inclusionality is a highly original and significant contribution to our understandings of life, the environment and people. His ideas challenge many of the assumptions on which Western ways of thinking have developed through the use of categorical systems of thought. Through the use of multi-media forms of communication Rayner demonstrates the significance of his ideas for a wide range of disciplines and for the education of individuals in community.

Professor Jack Whitehead

Professor, Liverpool Hope University, Liverpool, UK.

What I greatly admire about Alan Rayner's endeavours is his courage and flair in bringing the critical intellect and the creative imagination into productive relation in such an energizing manner.

Lindsay Clarke

Whitbread Award-winning novelist

NaturesScope

Unlocking Our Natural Empathy and Creativity.

An inspiring new way of relating to our natural

origins and one another through 'natural inclusion'

Alan Rayner

BOOKS

Winchester, UK
Washington, USA

First published by O-Books, 2011
O-Books is an imprint of John Hunt Publishing Ltd., Laurel House, Station Approach,
Alresford, Hants, SO24 9JH, UK
office1@o-books.net
www.o-books.com

For distributor details and how to order please visit the 'Ordering' section on our website.

Text copyright Alan Rayner 2010

ISBN: 978 1 84694 980 7

A CIP catalogue record for this book is available from the British Library.

Design: Tom Davies

Printed in the UK by CPI Antony Rowe
Printed in the USA by Offset Paperback Mfrs, Inc

We operate a distinctive and ethical publishing philosophy in all
areas of our business, from our global network of authors to
production and worldwide distribution.

CONTENTS

About the Author

Alan Rayner is a naturalist who uses art, poetry and a new kind of mathematics, as well as rigorous science to enquire and communicate about our natural human neighbourhood. He was born in Nairobi, Kenya in 1950, educated at King's College, Cambridge and is currently a Reader at the University of Bath. He has published over 150 scientific articles, 6 formal scientific books (including *Degrees of Freedom–Living in Dynamic Boundaries*), and six e-books. He was President of the British Mycological Society in 1998 and has been a Miller Visiting Research Professor at the University of California, Berkeley.

Preview

For thousands of years we have tried to study, interpret and teach ourselves *about* Nature from our own point of view, through the lenses of our telescopes, microscopes and binocular eyesight directed outwards. We see a rigidly framed objective picture 'out there' that does not include ourselves yet upon which we project our own image and psychology. This one-way view has brought us into profound conflict with our natural origins and one another. 'NaturesScope' evokes a different view, *from* Nature, which brings human beings and the world into empathic mutual relationship. It assists us in enquiring imaginatively and creatively into how to turn the narrowed-down objective worldview around and see ourselves and our world through nature's fluid lens of mutual inclusion. People who have experienced this view of natural inclusion have found it a source of profound inspiration.

List of Images

Author's Preface

On the morning of Tuesday 30th June, 2009, I had a strong sense of history, both in the making and in the breaking, as I prepared to give a talk on 'Fungus-Tree Relationships' in the very place where Darwin & Wallace's paper on the 'Origin of Species' was first presented. My anxiety was not dispelled when recent President of the Linnaean Society, Professor David Cutler, warned all speakers that Darwin's eyes would be following them, from his enormous portrait on the wall! I addressed Darwin's portrait and expressed my delight in his insight, as a naturalist, into the evolutionary kinship of all life, but my dismay in his rationalistic explanation of this kinship as a consequence of 'natural selection, or the preservation of favoured races in the struggle for life'.

For I knew that the key message I wished to get across was that we need to move on from the Darwin-inspired habit of thinking about trees, fungi and indeed all life forms as if they are self-centred objects, subject to the selective influence of external force. If we want to evolve more sensitive and sensible ways of working with them, we need to consider the dynamic context of the complex, variable, fluid neighbourhoods they truly and naturally inhabit. I also knew that practitioners who work with real life are intuitively already all too aware of this truth, yet may find it difficult to be explicit about as they struggle with standardized rules, regulations and formulae imposed by a rationalistic mindset fearful of uncertainty.

How had I come to find myself in this situation?

I have been working on the development of a way of explaining evolution that doesn't suffer from the inconsistencies, paradoxes and adverse social, psychological and environmental implications of natural selection theory. I have called this new explanation 'natural inclusion'. Briefly, 'natural inclusion' can be described as 'the co-creative transformation of all through all in receptive space'.

I was alerted to the problems of natural selection theory—arising from the fact that the logic of 'selection' isn't actually 'natural' – by my many years of research on fungi and trees. I found that it wasn't possible adequately to understand the variable dynamic relationships and patterns of development of these organisms by regarding them as if they are self-centred objects. Moreover, to do so may result in damaging instead of beneficial methods of managing trees and their cultivation, which neglect the ecological context in which they thrive – for example by growing trees in adverse soils and locations, intolerance of risk, and pruning and felling them inaptly or unnecessarily. It makes more sense to think of trees and fungi – and indeed all organisms – as naturally variable neighbourhoods or *flow-forms*, whose development and interrelationships are sensitively dependent on their environmental situation. Experienced practitioners are often more intuitively aware of this situation than theorists who attempt to formulate standard codes of practice.

During the 1990s I gradually realized that these problems weren't confined to understanding trees and fungi but extended to how we human beings have mostly come to study, interpret and educate ourselves about the natural world and our place in it, based on a rationalistic, 'whole way of thinking' that promotes profound intolerance and conflict. This rationalistic thinking is founded in the supposition – deeply embedded in orthodox mathematics, science, governance and theology – that matter can be isolated from space. There is neither any evidence for this supposition, nor does it make consistent sense of our experience. But the damaging effect that it has is to compel us to draw an imaginary hard line or 'discontinuity' between our individual 'selves' and our natural neighbourhood. This imaginary hard line is at the root of conflict between all kinds of intolerant fundamentalist ideologies as well as a source of great difficulty in predicting and relating to environmental change.

Partly as a result of this realization, I stopped actively researching fungal and tree biology in 1999 and started to research in an interdisciplinary way with any artists, mathematicians, natural scientists, engineers, sociologists, therapists, theologians, philosophers, educators, former drug addicts, managers, organizations – and most especially Bath University undergraduates – I could find who shared my view that we have been teaching ourselves to think in a way that is socially, environmentally and psychologically damaging. This research led to the development of a new ecological and evolutionary understanding of natural energy flow called 'inclusionality', from which the concept of 'natural inclusion' arose. Inclusionality is the understanding of all natural form as flow-form – an energetic configuration of space in figure and figure in space, such that space, as a receptive (non-resistive) presence, is not assumed to be discontinuous (i.e. to stop at discrete boundary limits). Unlike rationalistic thinking, inclusionality therefore does not assume or impose completion at any scale of natural organisation and so is a source of deep tolerance and love of natural variety.

I am continuing to research the implications of inclusionality, and how most effectively to communicate this understanding to a wider community, along as many avenues and with as many like-minded people as I can. I include art, poetry and a new kind of mathematics, as well as scientific observation and inference in my approach.

I want this book to be a source of interest and pleasure for anyone who cares about our human place in the natural world. My aim is to provide an *opening* for imagination and reflection, not a scholarly course of instruction. *I can only explicate my perceptions and reasoning for opening the door into natural inclusionality in my personally unique way, using whatever means I have available to me, and invite others across the threshold if they wish.* I have therefore drawn together a variety of essays, poems, paintings and accounts from previous works, many of which can be found via the Internet, and laced these together with some new writing to *reveal* what I hope will be a rich and exciting yet ultimately coherent unfolding of the meaning of natural inclusion. This cannot, therefore, be a straightforward account from beginning to conclusion, but more like a river for the reader to navigate in much the same way that a canoeist might, from upper reaches to sea. There will be rapids and shallows, meanders and deep pools, iterations and re-iterations, complex entanglements and smooth passages.

Alan Rayner

Contents Summary

I have organized this book in an unusual way, which I hope will help to invite the more imaginative kind of thinking that I think is necessary to appreciate the source of human empathy and creativity in natural creativity. It is only by exercising our extraordinary human imagination that I believe it is possible to liberate ourselves from the oppressive unnatural confinements of oppositional logic that can lead us, like Charles Darwin, to regard life as a competitive 'struggle for existence' in which 'only the fittest survive'. Most especially, we need to be able to imagine how it feels to be in the place of another – an ability called empathy, which is the deep source of human compassion and creativity. But to be truly liberating this imagination needs also to be tempered and disciplined by realistic considerations of what is consistent with evidence and what makes consistent sense. In other words, we need to combine the analytical and linguistic linear-processing capabilities of the left hemisphere of our human brains with the intuitive, pictorial, parallel-processing capabilities of the right hemisphere. We need to combine Science and the Humanities, not drive them into the apartheid between 'Two Cultures' famously diagnosed by C.P. Snow.

I have therefore populated the book with examples of exercising my own imagination in the form of poetry, prose and painting, as well as carefully argued text. I am not trying to 'show off my talent' – if anything, I feel rather embarrassed by its lack of erudition and exposure of my own mental blocks – but rather to tickle the reader's imagination. Poetic expression especially strikes me as a way of bridging between the articulate and picturing mind in touch with our deepest feelings. Each of the following reflections therefore begins with one or more poems – or quote from a poet – relating to the theme in question. The examples of my own paintings are similarly used as a kind of 'visual poetry', neither completely abstract nor completely representational, to illustrate these themes in what I hope will be an evocative way. To reduce the cost of the book, they are printed in black and white. Original colour versions can be found at www.inclusionality.org and www.inclusional-research.org.

0. Opening – The Need for Care
An introduction to the core theme of the book and its psychological, social and environmental relevance

1. What Happens When Ice Melts:
The Need for a Global Warming of Human Thought
A reflection upon how we have imposed a frozen frame of abstract logic upon nature, how this leads us to lose sight of the primary inducer of fluid movement and co-creativity and how our current fears of human-caused climate change could both hinder and help us to melt this frame into a more empathic understanding of human nature within nature.

2. Loving Our Natural Neighbourhood as Self
A consideration of the benefits of logically and mathematically transfiguring our perception of 'self-identity' from discrete automatons at odds with nature to distinct natural inclusions with local, figural and non-local spatial aspects.

3. The Meaning of Natural Variety
An exposition of the evolutionary origins and significance of natural variety and why a mechanism of selective favouritism cannot sustain or generate it.

4. Fluidity as Tolerance
An appreciation of fluid tolerance as vital to evolutionary creativity, not just as an aid to putting up with difference.

5. Creativity at Heart

An account of the deep origins of human creativity within natural creativity.

0. Opening – The Need for Care

Creative Intention

My intention in this opening reflection is to begin to uncover the core theme of this book and show how and why an appreciation of natural creativity requires an attitude of mind that is careful, both in being *respectful* and *compassionate* towards what might otherwise seem to be opposing points of view. The opening poem alludes to an actual human condition called 'unilateral neglect' which follows damage to one brain hemisphere or other (most usually the right hemisphere) and results in inattention to one half of the visual field (the left half, if the right hemisphere is damaged). In a similar kind of way, the predomination of analytical over intuitive thought, or vice versa, may involve inattention to or lack of communication with what the other half is offering. The second poem relates to a mental condition, called 'Achilles Syndrome', in which the creative giftedness, sensitivity and compassion that are sourced in accepting human vulnerability can become transformed into a morbid and paralyzing fear of failure.

Neglect
At last I know
What's been wrong for me
That absence of care
Which leaves you wondering where you are
As the wind howls
Through broken windows to your soul
Framing a derelict construction
In the backyard of inattention

At last I know
What's been wrong for us

That plain-speaking nonsense
Which leaves out what's within us
As the mind growls
Against the disruption of its face
Painted on the wall that stands
In the foreground of rejection

Where two sides can never meet
Each seeking the other's complete defeat
In hollow victory
Where wind howls
As mind growls
Against the dying of the light

Until, at last, a loophole's found
Where lonely figure finds its place
In ground
Where deserted ground extends its space
Through figure
Each finding life
In the care of the other
Where what's good for the life and love of both
Is good for the life and love of each
Despite appearances that seem to teach
The need to preserve against the other's reach

Achilles Heal
A gap breathed space
Into the fortress
Of a soul walled in
By dreaming of Absolute security
In its individual completeness

Elevated above some baseline standard

Of soles firmly planted
At odds with one as another
In foundations of quicksand
Set fast in cement

How quickly this dreaming
Would fade
In less than a lifeline
Of certain anchorage

When doubt made its fearful question
Of presence felt
In a blow below the belt
That crippled unbending fixture
Into sharply wrought relief

Curved into some new and ancient
Awareness
Where no One could still compete
When stilled by its own completeness
Of idolized concrete

Inviolate to all but its own violation
Of unfelt presence
So deeply disconcerted
By no sense of nonsense
In the absence of its motherhood

Through which to find communion
From sole to soul
Unblockaded
By proud pretension

A humility restored

To Faith in individual failure
As sure and omnipresent sign
Of love in human nature

Opening all ways
To unending Recreation
In the very Shadow of Tragedy
The Community Play of Foolish Genius

Beyond restrictive lessons
In Schools of Guilty Thought
That burden the bleating Heart
With endless ways to blame and shame
By reserving the right for One Alone
To claim superiority

Closure

All the signs are that thousands of years of abstract thought have led modern human cultures to become neglectful to the point where we no longer know how or why to care for one another and the natural world. Somehow, many of us have managed to convince ourselves that our human self-interest differs from the interests of our natural neighbourhood. At the core of this conviction is the fallacy that we can draw a hard line – an absolute discontinuity – between what is inside and what is outside any form or figure, which defines it as an independent 'subject' or 'object' with its own centre. No sooner is this hard line drawn, then all the familiar trappings of human trouble and strife that are embedded in the divisive logical foundations of orthodox mathematics and theology, objective science and hierarchical governance become reinforced. We get drawn into opposing: black *against* white, left *against* right, darkness *against* light, life *against* death, mind *against* matter, human *against* non-human, one *against* many, positive *against* negative, material *against* immaterial, love *against* hate, right *against* wrong, truth *against* falsehood, good *against* evil, matter *against* anti-matter, ego *against* Shadow, individual *against* collective, male *against* female, nature *against* nurture, holism *against* reductionism etc. We allow no room for resolution of the conflict in their midst. We take sides, each regarding the other as its enemy and declare 'you're either with me or against me'. And when we tire of the bipolar war between different worlds, we seek not to appreciate how they all contribute to the vitality of a rich and heterogeneous nature, but how to merge them seamlessly together in a unified 'Whole' of no difference, no boundary save the one that somehow paradoxically defines it as a closed entity in its own right.

Somewhere absolutely vital gets omitted from our consideration when we define one thing as not another thing through the ancient Greek 'Law of the Excluded Middle'. This is somewhere that we need to take immense care not to overlook, if we are not to fall into the trap that leads us not to care for one another and the natural world that sustains and brings us to life. We are prone to overlook it because, as terrestrial, omnivorous, bipedal apes unable to digest plant cellulose but equipped with binocular vision and opposable thumbs that enable us to catch and grasp, we are predisposed to view the geometry of our natural neighbourhood in an overly definitive way. We see 'boundaries' as the limits of definable 'objects' and 'space' as 'nothing' – a gap or absence outside and between these objects. This impression gets reinforced by the inhibitory influence of our frontal brain lobes and the contrast between our verbally articulate, linear-processing left and inarticulate, parallel-processing right cerebral hemispheres. Only if we are somehow to 'marry' our focused forward vision with our all-round intuitive comprehension of where we are in the world, through opening the communication channel (ostensibly, the 'corpus callosum' between brain hemispheres) may we be able poetically to override this impression and gain the deeper evolutionary understanding that this book seeks to reveal.

Openness

This *vital presence* that we need to become aware of by opening our minds to its creative possibilities is literally everywhere, in front of our noses and up our nostrils. We are prone to overlook or obscure it by regarding it as *nothing,* an immaterial, physical absence. But in reality it is nothing less than the *limitless physical presence of space as receptive openness* within, around and throughout the variably viscous natural flow-forms – the energetic configurations of space in figure and figure in space – that inhabit the cosmos, including ourselves. *Once aware of this receptive presence we recognize the impossibility of defining or measuring anything in absolute numerical terms anywhere, because all form has both a 'figural', energetic inner-outer interfacing or dynamic boundary, which makes it distinct, and a 'transfigural' – 'through the figure' – spatial reach that cannot be sliced or limited.* The trans-figural space throughout and beyond the figure pools it within the co-creative, influential neighbourhood of all others. Without it, figures become lifeless and loveless, stone-cold bodies, integral or fractional numbers and idealized geometric points, lines and solids. It is what has gone missing from our abstract perceptions of nature in terms of objective or subjective 'parts' and 'wholes'. Its return brings our conception of figures back to life and love in the naturally creative evolutionary dance of figural and transfigural presences in each other's inseparable company and mutual influence. We escape the confinement and inconsistencies of the definitive *fixed boundary logic* of 'one opposed to other' that has held our imagination to ransom for millennia, and move on to a more natural form of reasoning in the *fluid boundary logic* or *fluid transfigural logic* (see later) of each in the other's mutual influence.

As William Wordsworth recognized almost 200 years ago, 'in nature everything is distinct, yet nothing defined into absolute, independent singleness'. The discrete (completely definable) abstract numerical units of conventional mathematics and assumed to exist by every objectivist science theory – including Darwin's adversarial notion of 'natural selection, or the preservation of favoured races in the struggle for life' – cannot and do not exist in the variably fluid cosmos we actually inhabit. Evolution cannot proceed through the paradoxical imposition of external, selectively judgemental force upon singular subject-objects. Evolution can only proceed through **natural inclusion** – *the co-creative, fluid dynamic transformation of all through all in receptive spatial context.*

Through the *natural inclusionality* of understanding all natural form as flow form, an energetic configuration of space in figure and figure in space, we can transform the divisive *abstract rationality* that teaches us not to care by attempting to preserve our individual selves against infinite odds. We can recognize the needless and tragic implications of Hamlet's rationalization:

> *To be or not to be, that is the question: whether 'tis nobler in the mind to suffer the slings and arrows of outrageous fortune, or to take arms against a sea of troubles, and by opposing end them?*

And find truth instead in:

Space – Your Final Dissolution
I am your final dissolution
The nurturer of your nature
That soothes and softens
As we live and breathe together

No gas-tight chamber doors
Designed to wall in
Or wall out your fears of devastation
Can exterminate me

You cannot live without me
You cannot die without me
I cannot find expression without you
You live in the breath of my inspiration
You die in the breath of my expiration
You die as you live
You live as you die
With me
Within and without

So, if you try to close me in
Or close me out
In your Manly human quest for Godly immortality
I cannot love you as you stir within my womb

I cannot assist you
I can only watch, impassively by
As you use me to destroy
Yourself

Or suffocate in the stasis
Of a never-ending, never-opening
Paralysis
That's no life for any one of us
Alone

So, please, bear with me
As I am alongside and within you
Take me in as I take you out
Certain only of the uncertainty
That recreates a rich and vibrant world
I am what life and death is all about

Rising and subsiding

In ever-flowing form
Living Light and Loving Darkness
Together

And:

Continual Re-Creation
Deep in the heart of everywhere
Resides the receptive space of somewhere
That yearns to bear her offspring
Pulsing with life's rhythms
From what she has drawn from beyond
Into where she generates from within
Her swirling cup
Of darkness in light surface
And light in deep darkness
That welcomes the spirit of masculine
Into the soul of feminine
And guides him on through
The confined fields of Eros
To that infinite expanse
Of open Agape
Only to return
Again and again
To creating together
In primordial womb
The one and the many
Those worlds without end
In a world without end
No end

And:

Holding Openness

You ask me who you are
To tell a story you can live your life by
A tail that has some point
That you can see
So that you no longer
Have to feel so pointless
Because what you see is what you get
If you don't get the meaning of my silence
Because you ain't seen nothing yet

You ask me for illumination
To cast upon your sauce of doubt
Regarding what your life is all about
To find a reason for existence
That separates the wrong
From righteous answer
In order to cast absence out
To some blue yonder
Where what you see is what you get
But you don't get the meaning of my darkness
Because you ain't seen nothing yet

You look around the desolation
Of a world your mined strips bare
You ask of me in desperation
How on Earth am I to care?
I whisper to stop telling stories
In abstract words and symbols
About a solid block of land out there
In which you make yourself a declaration
Of independence from thin air
Where what you see is what you get
When you don't get the meaning of my present absence

Because you ain't seen nothing yet

You ask of me with painful yearning
To resolve your conflicts born of dislocation
From the context of an other world out where
Your soul can wonder freely
In the presence of no heir
Where what you see is what you get
When you don't get the meaning of my absent presence
Because you ain't seen nothing yet

You ask me deeply and sincerely
Where on Earth can you find healing
Of the yawning gap between emotion
And the logic setting time apart from motion
In a space caught in a trap
Where what you see is what you get

And in a thrice your mind is reeling
Aware at last of your reflection
In a place that finds connection
Where your inside becomes your outside
Through a lacy curtain lining
Of fire, light upon the water

Now your longing for solution
Resides within and beyond your grasp
As the solvent for your solute
Dissolves the illusion of your past
And present future

Now your heart begins to thunder
Bursting hopeful with affection
Of living light for loving darkness

Because you ain't felt no thing yet

'Holding Openness' (Oil painting on canvas by Alan Rayner, 2005). *Light as a dynamic inclusion of darkness continually brings an endless diversity of flow-form to Life.*

Life, Love and Suffering – From Demanding Human Rights to Appreciating Human Needs

Theme
The source of our human capacity to suffer is also vital to our ability to live, love and be loved. By denigrating it, through an unrealistic aspiration to individual or collective autonomy, we aggravate rather than eliminate suffering. By acknowledging it, we allow compassionate wisdom and natural creativity to flourish in our midst.

Autonomous Denial

> *Breast cancer, I can now report, did not make me prettier or stronger, more feminine or spiritual. What it gave me, if you want to call this a 'gift', was a very personal, agonising encounter with*

an ideological force in American culture that I had not been aware of before – one that encourages us to deny reality, submit cheerfully to misfortune and blame only ourselves for our fate
[From 'Smile or Die: How Positive Thinking Fooled America and the World', by Barbara Ehrenreich, Granta, January 2010]

"This notion, which now involves seeing everything natural as an object, inert, senseless and detached from us, arose as part of the dualist vision of a split between body and soul. It was designed to glorify God by removing all competing spiritual forces from the realm of nature...Why do we still think like this? Why can't we be more realistic?" Mary Midgley, reviewing 'The Master and His Emissary: The Divided Brain and the Making of the Western World', by Iain McGilchrist in Saturday Guardian, 02/01/10.

You've got to ac-cent-tchu-ate the positive
Elim-my-nate the negative
Latch on to the affirmative
Don't mess with Mr In-between
Johnny Mercer (1944)

The way we human beings view our capacity to suffer and die profoundly affects the way we understand our relationships with one another and the natural world that we inhabit. Even, and perhaps especially, what many of us view as our most detached and rational ways of thinking may be more rooted in the psychology of fear than a realistic appraisal of our actual situation and natural neighbourhood.

A common way of dealing with something we fear is to try to ward it off or pretend that it doesn't exist or amounts to nothing. In the words of Robert Frost:

Nature does not complete things. She is chaotic. Man must finish, and he does so by making a garden and building a wall

In other words, we may try to eliminate the source of uncertainty and loss that we associate with pain and mortality by imposing the unnaturally definable order of a *'whole* way of thinking' on the wildness around and within ourselves. We aspire to be complete, self-sufficient individuals in our own right, capable of extending our dominion – or the dominion of One who we are prepared to subjugate ourselves to – to the edge of a completely knowable world in which we can preserve our safe passage forever. We then proceed to embed this aspiration in our logic, theology, science and systems of governance, to the point where we regard its reality as unquestionable. We might even have the temerity to declare that:

> *We hold these truths to be self-evident, that all men are created equal, that they are endowed by their Creator with certain unalienable Rights, that among these are Life, Liberty and the pursuit of Happiness.*

Alternatively, we may shift the notion of completeness and autonomy from individual to collective, holding that:

> *The whole is more than the sum of its parts* – Aristotle

and thereby subordinating the uniqueness of the particular to the requirements of the global in which it is supposedly inextricably embedded and connected, tangibly or intangibly, to all others.

The real truth, however, is that to sustain such ultimately paradoxical belief systems, we have to build them upon a logical foundation that is inconsistent with evidence and does not make consistent sense – the supposition that material form can either be isolated from or is co-extensive with space. For this to be true, space would have to be divisible or containable – that is, to stop and/or start at discrete boundary limits, like a sea detached from river or river detached from sea.

The river is within us; the sea is all about us – TS Eliot

This space I can imagine empty, but I cannot imagine the thing without the space – L. Wittgenstein

If natural form was purely material, it could consist of no more than a dimensionless point with no shape or size. If natural form was purely spatial, it would be featureless. If nature consisted purely of solid, massy particles and space wasn't a natural presence, nothing could move. If space was just an infinite emptiness surrounding discrete objects, there would be no place to situate an external source of force to move these objects around. If space wasn't within and throughout as well as around natural form, it wouldn't be possible for form to be distinguishable or to flow as liquid or gas or to have variable qualities of density, bounciness, flexibility and conductivity.

The attempt to impose definition on indeterminacy and degree and exception is about the straightest road to mischief I know of - very deeply worn, very well travelled
Marilynne Robinson, The Death of Adam: Essays on Modern Thought

In nature, everything is distinct, yet nothing defined into absolute, independent singleness – William Wordsworth

No man is an island, entire of it self – John Donne

Hence it is inescapable that the natural world of movement and mobility that we sense and inhabit cannot be defined completely into hard and fast categories. There is no absolutely closed form that we know of or can know of. Space is energetically included in form and form in space. Space is an indivisible, indefinable presence of openness everywhere, infinite at all scales, not an empty absence of definable presence within or outside the finite bounds of discrete, active and reactive material objects. In relationship with energetic form, space has a receptive quality that *induces* flow. In relationship with omnipresent space, energetic form has a responsive quality that enables it to flow into place.

This is the understanding of the creative evolutionary wildness of natural energy flow that has been called 'natural inclusionality', to distinguish it from the 'objective rationality' of definitive assumptions that underpin individualism and collectivism, reductionism and (w)holism. According to natural inclusionality, all natural form is variably viscous 'flow-form' – an energetic configuration of space in figure and figure in space. The inherently static logic of discrete definition, which excludes or unnaturally confines the continuous space throughout and beyond all natural distinguishable form, is thereby subsumed by a fluid logic of 'the including middle', where the latter is the seat of dynamic correspondence, not dichotomy, between local figural and non-local spatial presences. These presences combine in dynamically distinct but not isolated bodily identities as natural inclusions of 'everywhere' in 'somewhere'.

Inclusional Acceptance
Definitive thinking, driven perhaps most fundamentally by an understandable desire to prevent suffering by imposing an unnaturally discrete order on things, has a very unfortunate outcome, which actually aggravates instead of alleviates human distress and conflict. By treating suffering as the consequence of *imperfection*, viewed as any absence of regularity or 'spot of bother' either within or outside ourselves or natural neighbourhood, it seeks to restore order through the imposition of discrete limits – most often manifest in some form of defensive

wall. Since these limits serve 'positively' to preserve the 'ideal' autonomous perfection of individual or group, whatever source of wildness – from volcanic eruption to 'foreign' invasion – appears capable of eroding them is viewed 'negatively' as a flaw or adversary that we must battle against to survive. Yet these very same limits also cut us off from what we actually depend on for dear life, whether we perceive this as Nature, God or both.

To be or not to be, that is the question: whether 'tis nobler in the mind to suffer the slings and arrows of outrageous fortune, or to take arms against a sea of troubles, and by opposing end them? – Hamlet

So we get caught in a double bind that holds us solely responsible for our behaviour – whereupon we either only have ourselves to blame when we suffer (i.e. there is something wrong *with* us if we suffer – pain and death are the wages of sin, insubordination, bad genes, bad attitude etc) or we blame God/Nature/Evil for making it/allowing it to happen. This leads us to disparage either those who suffer (with whom we have no sympathy because it's their own stupid 'fault') or that/those which seem to inflict or allow suffering. One way and another, we try not to admit (i.e. to exclude/deny) suffering by removing or sealing our bodily selves off from what we perceive as its source. But always at the root of such disparagement/inadmission is the groundless abstract rationalistic assumption that autonomy is 'real', a product either of our self-definition as discontinuous material bodies split apart from space, or group definition within a seamless whole entire of itself.

Natural inclusionality radically changes our perception of the source of human vulnerability and recognizes this also as vital to our ability to live, love and be loved. This source is nothing less than the receptive space and creative potential that all definitive ways of thinking intransigently ignore or deny.

With the recognition that suffering is an inescapable implication of our natural inclusion of and in receptive space, vital to our ability to live, love and be loved, comes a very different attitude. Suffering is not directly attributable to anyone or anything's 'fault', as such, and so should not be disparaged or denied, but alleviated through the receptive and needful capacity for love and care in which it is sourced. We move from angrily declaring our autonomous right to be happy and not to suffer, or serenely denying the distinctness of our bodily selves, to accepting our receptive human need for love and care. This 'need' is our receptive 'negative strength' through which we sustain our lives, not our despicable 'positive weakness'.

This is why the constant demand for 'positivity' and disdain for 'negativity' (as an admission of human need) evident in modern culture is deeply counter-inclusional. Natural inclusionality entails the dynamic balancing of 'positive' and 'negative' flow and counterflow under each other's reciprocal influence through the continuity of receptive space, not the battle for dominion of one against the other as discontinuous forces. To sustain this balance it is vital to include 'Mr In-Between' as the dynamic interfacing that both distinguishes each from other and provides spatial passage between them.

You've got to ack-knowl-age ev-ry positive
Affirm ev-ry negative
Grant Space of the Inclusional
And Inter-face with Mr In-between
Roy Reynolds 2010

1. What Happens When Ice Melts: The Need for a Global Warming of Human Thought

Creative Intention

Here I consider the implications of how imposing a frozen frame of abstract logic upon nature leads us to lose sight of the primary source and inducer of fluid movement and co-creativity. I reflect further upon how our current fears of human-caused climate change could both hinder and help us to melt this frame into a more empathic understanding of human nature within nature.

Catching the Sun
Where would the sun be
With nowhere to catch its rays
And spin them into Life
Throbbing in receptive bodies
Responsive to warmth
Conveyed in light too deep in shade
For human eyes to see?

Where would we be
Without a place to call our home
Receptive to influx
Responsive to neighbours
Each gathering harvest to pass on
Through channels unseen?

Where would cosmos be
Without somewhere to call its own
Reflecting in its mind's eyes
All that comes and goes in flows
Through the natural communion

Of spirit and soul
That expresses its passion
Through bodies seen and felt?

Nowhere and everywhere
Without a womb or heart
To revolve into Life

Catching Cold
When all becomes crystal
Clear in the mind
Life comes to stand still
Sharp and unkind
Where rivers of diamonds
Cut slots into landscape
Without caring to wind
Round hillsides in valleys
But compete crotch to crotch
To be seen as top notch

Words become viral
Without pausing to spiral
But burst forth in splutters
And under-breath mutters
Transmitted between shudders
Not in milk drunk from udders
Because flow can't be trusted
When all becomes rusted
Into points of corrosion
Plotting lines of erosion
Between one mind and other
Deprived of their Mother

Who can cure these destructions

Of life caught in ructions
Between each locked apart
In freeze-framed art
Where no warmth can travel
Allowing bodies to unravel
From their in the spot race
To find their selves in fond embrace

No-one, no-where
Unless
A way is found between here and there
Which is ever-present, every-where
Never growing older
And without cold shoulder

The Humility of the Valley
Life doesn't strive
To secure its foundation
Upon the rocky serrations of the High-minded
Where Men build castles in the air
To furnish that false sense of superiority
Which comes from the pretence
Of overlooking all around
To the edge of infinity

Life thrives
In the seclusion of the valleys
Where dampness accumulates
In the earthy humidity
Of humility
Warmly tucked in
To the bed of sea and land
Rich with variety
Exuding

Intruding
Out and into the cosiness
Of each lovingly enveloped
In the other's influence

Wisdom cannot be found
On peaks of adaptive fitness
Running with Red Queens
But only in that radiant depth
That reaches everywhere
Through the heart of somewhere

Frozen Field

It seems so long ago now, that the Snow Queen cast the spell that held her subjects spellbound, locked in a cold frame of false security with pretensions to freedom. So long ago and yet it seems like only yesterday. That's always the way when you abstract time from place and schedule your life at a frantic pace, always busy, without pause for reflection. Competing against the clock and one another by any means to ensure you're all that's left behind when the end comes. You consume each slice of time with each slice of space, all neatly set out in cubical cubicles with no room for ease with your life in a squeeze. Until at last you come to the end and realize that life's passed you by. And now you're a dead cert for staying a head when your heart would feel better for taking love in instead and melting your ice in the flow that passes all understanding through all in a limitless pool whose surface suffices without polish to gloss over infinite depth.

'Vernal Illuminations' (Oil painting on Board, by Alan Rayner, 1999). *Separate sexes of hazel and alder catkins, and hermaphrodite flowers of celandines illuminate springtime emergence from winter darkness. The impenetrable, mirror surface of a lake of clear tear water contains both shadows and reflections but admits no insight within its straight-edged, arum-lined, and sinuous boundaries. Grief is fathomless, imponderable, but not without respite or hope cascading from the conciliation of polarities.*

Busyness, As Usual

He looked up at me, with dulled, mournful eyes
Torn momentarily from his job in hand
By my tacit intrusion
'What do you want?'
He asked

'I want you to see through what you're doing'
I replied
'So that you can have a life

Beyond your passing of time from cradle to grave
Where you no longer need to feel so oppressed
By such conflict of interest
Between who you are
And who you think you are
Once told that you must
Abandon all trust
And find hope instead
In infinite dread
And so turn away
From the bright light of day
That calls you to play
And work Hell for Leather
In Order to tether
The love of your life
To trouble and strife

Can't you see if you will
Spit out that sweet pill
What joy we could find
To save humankind
From suffering the pain
Of endless disdain
At the hands of the story
That calls all to glory
By weeding them out
Without casting a clout
From where they belong
In the summer of song
Which draws all its zest
From the silence of rest
In winter's warm furring
And nightjar's churring
At the slide of the day

And the smell of the May
That blossoms from furling
With petals uncurling
From deep in their womb
Protected in gloom

All you have to do
Is dissolve all that glue
That keeps you attached
To your egg once you've hatched
And open up space
From that place of disgrace
Stuck in the corner
Like little Jack Horner
With dunce's cap on
Until with aplomb
You stick up your digit
And scramble to fidget
Your way out of limbo
By marrying that Bimbo
Who won't trouble to question
Your harsh indigestion
From having to swallow
What can only bring sorrow
From your sovereign right
To run from your fright
And stiffen in vertex
To save your day from yielding to night'

He looked back at me, in disbelief
And his eyes welled up with the waters of grief
As his mouth opened wide and said
'I've no time for that, it's over my head
Now please leave me alone

With the life that I own
It's time for my bed'

There is something about the nature of infinity that defeats the purpose of a controlling mind: a permissiveness that makes room for all kinds of unpredictable possibilities in the long run. It is this permissiveness that the sovereign mind seeks to reign in by reining in, within the confines of abstractly-defined limits. Only within such limits can there be no escape from the mind's dominion into the 'wild' outside.

So it has been, for millennia, that the desire of human nature to control nature in order to sustain order has sought all kinds of fiendish devices to divide and rule by walling itself in, against the assault of unimaginable odds. But in so doing, it has only succeeded in defeating itself, by ruling out what is vital to the very possibility of living, loving and learning in a continually evolving world and cosmos. Now, as what's been ruled out makes its presence felt in the guise of what's perceived by the sovereign as the unwelcome repercussions of its own power in the form of runaway climate change, panic is setting in, instead of the deeper reflection needed to recognize what's gone missing from its account book. Like the stone that claims sole responsibility for the ripple in a pool, with no consideration for the nature of what it's immersed in, the sovereign seeks to single out whatever or whoever within its reign can be held to account and brought down low. Without pausing for a moment to consider the influence of what's been left out in the act of singling out, the scapegoat's found and tormented into submission within a cage of arbitrary limits called 'targets'. Meanwhile, Louis Pasteur, founding father of the 'germ theory of disease', who finally admitted 'the microbe is nothing, the terrain is all', turns in his grave. And government spending on 'defence' hugely outweighs its investment in 'the environment' – the estranged territory that somehow isn't considered to include 'social and economic interests'.

So, as the ice blocks melt from glaciers and snow caps, heralding who *really* knows what – whether it be warming or chilling or more of the same – the freeze-frames of sovereign mathematical abstraction are wheeled in, complete with hockey-stick graphs, to delineate what will come to pass unless we take to task that criminal class within, which commits the grievous sin that consigns us to the bin of extinguished life. All hands are called to the pump of what's in the foreground of attention, whilst all else fades into the background of inattention. That neglected natural human neighbourhood, where infinity resides, is cared for less and less as we seek to clear the mess that comes from neglecting it by ruling it out.

Tired of Waiting

I'm so tired
Tired of waiting
For a world to turn itself around
From continually revolving
In opposition to its motion
That blocks its circulation
In polarized debate

I can't wait
For the debate to abate
And stop its endless promotion
Of power-hungry clods
To positions where they stifle
Those truly gifted
With generosity to share

Why must those who care
From the depths of their sensitivity
To an uncertain kind of truth

That flows in all through all
Suffer endless humiliation
At the hands of those who call
Themselves successful
In a world that gives them clout?

Where there is no room for doubt
No space to air the possibility
Of living free from grout
That fixes tiles to walls
In rectilinear rankings
Of vertical ascent
To a tall story

From whose lofty penthouse
The ghost of high office
Watches out
Relentlessly
For anyone who dares to question
Or fall fearfully short of satisfying
The hard-edged logic of His restrictive practice
That knows no soft caress
And so couldn't care less

Whilst everywhere around
Throughout the quaking ground
Where reality floods in
To shake the certainty out of order
With violent protestations
That open space for reconciliation
Of one will with another
In a world where none can smother
The life that flows through all
And finds itself again

In the frail wonderings of compassion

No, I cannot bear to wait much longer
For the retirement of that force
That batters into thrall
The love that lives within us all
And turns the world around

Bowled Over
High up at the bottom of a bowl
Rimmed with ridges and cusps
Seeped through by blue rippling
Descending from ice-cap

A vast, steep-sided arena
Roaring with waterfalls
And fast-flowing river
Laced with low woodland
Filled with flowers
And rocky outcrops

I've never seen such a scene
Except in dreams
And imaginings of Lothlorien

A trail of enchantment
Moist, mossy and silvered with birch
Calling to continue
From rapture to rapture

Until a howl of foreboding
From a wolf
That turns out to be dog
Standing sentinel

But tethered beside the path
Warns to turn around

Before the ice is reached
Falling short
By a hundred or two metres
But never mind

The return seems longer than the coming
Even walking at the double
To carry clear of unknown trouble
Where wilderness strains at the leash
To make itself felt

Beyond the din
That begrudges mortal sin
For venturing so boldly
To invade its privacy

'Bowled Over' (Oil painting on canvas by Alan Rayner, 2008).

Spate Attack
I am a river damned to bursting point
Required by your close confinement
To down regulate my outflow
To a pitiful trickle
When I long to flood
And see you flailing in my excesses

Not because I want to drown you
But because I want to drown the din
Of your inconsideration
For what I can bring

To bear down upon your pallid protestations
Of exception from circumstance
That cruelly deny my loving influence
So that you can take one another apart
In death-defying leaps of soulless mentality
Into the hard ground of your unreality
Where life feeds the pungent corpse of your annihilation

No, I don't want to drown you
But how I yearn to see you swim
What a fine splash you'd make!

Pooled together in my liquidity
Taken up in common spirit
Where all resolve to solve is gone
Rendered needless by your oblivion
Of all that you have placed to stand in the way
Of your dearest, loving Mother

EnTrance to the Limitless Pool

For thousands of years humanity has held itself under the spell of a frozen field in which life is a battle between subjects and objects acting upon and reacting to one another in a desperate struggle to preserve their self-centres against infinite odds. This book seeks to liberate us from this thraldom by melting the ice of an intransigent way of thinking that gets in the way of our creativity, mutual understanding and trust and appreciation of one another and Nature. At the core of this intransigence is the fallacy that a discrete limit or 'discontinuity' can exist between the inside and outside of any natural form. This fallacy results in the mental imposition of a rigid geometric structure – whether that of a three-dimensional cube or surface of a sphere – upon what can really only be the infinite depth and openness of natural space. This structure is the frozen frame of space, the fixed 'field' that we have built in to our objective logic, mathematics, language, science and theology, which we have increasingly allowed literally to rule our lives through the device of overarching sovereign power. In our subservience to it, which gives us a false sense of freedom and security, we draw ourselves into profound conflict and an ecologically and evolutionarily unsustainable way of life that there is no escape from until and unless we begin to melt its hard-line boundaries.

Melting the frozen field of isolated form into the limitless pool of natural flow-form has been the hopeful intent of my work, along with a few like-minded souls, over the last ten years. Together, by bringing space from the empty background into the open foreground of our attention, we have been seeking what I can perhaps best describe as an *involution* of the damaging way that so many of us have been taught to think. We call this involution 'inclusionality' and find in it what we consider to be a general truth that transforms the 'part-truths' of conventional ration-ality into a more life-like configuration.[1]

Within this limitless pool and its vital inhabitants we find an understanding that for us brings hope of a more creative, sustainable and loving future for humanity and our companions.

But in no way do we underestimate just what an enormous upheaval this may bring for the way we imagine and live our lives. To sustain this understanding depends on the *imaginative* capacity to hold *both* the *figural* (local energetic configuration of space) *and transfigural* (non-local continuous depth/openness of space) *simultaneously* and *dynamically* (i.e. fluidly) in mind. One then 'sees' in the mind's eye the 'warm geometry' of a continually reconfiguring, variably viscous, dancing evolutionary flow of natural form as space in figure and figure in space. In essence this dynamic, mutually inclusive interplay of the fluidly figural (energetic) and omnipresent transfigural (space) is very simple and should be effortless to envisage. But within the cultural context of habitually 'hard-lining' things as complete, abstract, idealized figures it may require considerable effort, and there is always a tendency to default to the purely figural imagery (i.e. to 'lose imaginative sight' of the transfigural space). It may take even more imagination, together with a huge breadth and depth of scholarly knowledge and intellect, to envisage the *implications* of this imagery for understanding our natural neighbourhood and to appreciate how this involutes (turns outside-in) the freeze-framed, oppositional concepts of abstract rationality into the fluid understandings of complementary reciprocity offered by natural inclusionality.

The following simple exercise might help you appreciate the difference between the hard-line, space-cutting view of discontinuous models and fluid-line understanding of natural inclusionality and transfigurality. Draw an outline of two figures using a dotted line on a plain sheet of paper. The 'paper' stretched to infinity would represent what in the transfigural geometry developed by Lere Shakunle is called 'Omni-space' (Shakunle and Rayner, 2008, 2009). The space within each figure represents 'Intra-Space', the space between figures 'Inter-space' and the space transcending the figures' permeable and dynamic boundaries 'Trans-Space'. You can see how the continuous non-local space everywhere ('omni-space') is locally configured into distinctive, but *not discrete* regions. In the way that you have drawn them, the figures are not contiguous (connected), and so their 'intra-spaces' can only communicate through the 'inter-space' and 'trans-space' between and permeating their boundaries as *energetic interfacings* and *restraining influences* (not *restrictive* material *definitions* or external *forces*). Nonetheless, they still inhabit the same limitless pool of omni-space everywhere. If you were now to draw the figures closer together, so that their boundaries connect and coalesce at one or more points, their intra-space now becomes continuous. On the other hand, if you were to take a pair of scissors and cut around the dotted lines, the figures will drop out of their spatial context as discontinuous individual entities. This is what discontinuous models of reality effectively do – they treat boundaries as cut-out zones between discrete inner realms and outer realms, instead of dynamic relational interfacings through which these realms remain continuous through trans-space.

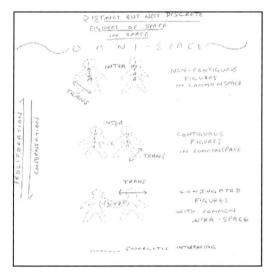

'**Figures of Space**' (Pencil sketch by Alan Rayner, 2010). *This sketch illustrates the dynamic relationships between figural flow-forms*

as energetic configurations of space in figure and figure in space. It also serves to distinguish the natural inclusional dynamic relationship between distinct but not discrete flow-forms both from reductive schemas that cut off inner from outer spatial realms and from connectivistic and wholistic schemas where individual dynamic locality is eschewed from a seamless, purely figural whole. Since the cartoons can only represent an instantaneous 'slice' through the figures, the dotted lines shouldn't be taken to represent 'sieves' but more the seething 'fluid mosaic' that constitutes real biological membranes (as well as all kinds of other 'surfaces' that appear smooth, fixed and complete from afar, but are revealed as fluidly energetic with closer inspection – like the sea viewed from the perspective of an astronaut and a swimmer). A very simple example of what is represented in the cartoon can also be seen between surface-tense droplets of water condensing on a surface. As they expand and come into proximity their tensely curved inner-outer interfacings first touch and then coalesce in a visible rush as each flows reciprocally into the other and the tension of their boundaries is released (Aaaaaaah!).

There is a historical pattern that repeats itself again and again through different kinds of local or non-local denial of the other, when the receptive presence of 'transfigural space' and corresponding responsive-reflective presence of 'dynamic interfacings/boundaries' is *neglected* through inadequate mental imagery of one kind or another:

Primordial wishy-washiness –> Rigid Definition –> Abstract Reductionism/Pluralism/Dualism/Fragmentedness –> De-definition –> Wishy-washiness –> Re-definition –> Holism/Monism/Oneness/Wholeness –>?

By excising/occluding the middle, rationalistic 'left hemisphere' perception becomes satisfied that it has completely accounted for Nature, by defining everything as a discrete material body within a discrete frame of space/time, and in so doing liberated humanity from the imprecise 'wishy-washiness' of 'right hemisphere perception'. Nature is divided up into innumerable, discontinuous, purely material parts and wholes that can be ruled into order according to the Laws laid down by a single sovereign authority. The upshot is reductionism and monotheism. 'Right hemisphere perception', meanwhile, recognizes the limitations of this reductive view and seeks to remove the definitive boundary limits imposed by it. The reductive view vehemently opposes this seeming assault on its integrity (which comes with a false and paradoxical sense of absolute security and freedom) by reinforcing its boundary limits as much as it can. But if it feels the discomfort that arises from its restrictive definitions, it may eventually be unable to resist collapsing into the nihilistic, angst-less, no-self world of wishy-washiness (nirvana/ La La Land) coming from pure right-hemisphere perception. Once in this no-self world, however, left hemisphere perception may spring back into action to recapture a sense of local definition (completeness) at the global scale of the 'Whole' as 'Oneness' (i.e. the rigid definition gets shifted from individual to collective, microcosm to macrocosm), and sticks there. Meanwhile, the 'third way' of 'each fluidly in the influence of the other' through transfigural space gets overlooked in the adversarial dialectic of mutual contradiction between the 'Many' and the 'One'.

If transfigural space is imaginatively included, however, we get:

Primordial wishy-washiness –> Fluid Distinction –> Natural Inclusionality/ Transfigurality/Three-in-one locality (somewhere) in non-locality (everywhere)

In a world of endless co-creativity. The inclusion of 'Trans-Space' makes all the difference between the morbidity of the 'frozen field' and the vitality of the 'limitless pool'.

2. Loving Our Natural Neighbourhood as Self

Creative Intention

Here I consider the creative benefits of logically and mathematically transfiguring our perception of 'self-identity' from discrete automatons at odds with nature to distinct receptive, reflective and responsive natural inclusions with local, figural and non-local spatial aspects. I show how this entails a transformation in our understanding of physical reality from discrete objective categories to distinctive flow-forms.

Imaginative Turn, 1/1/2010

How tiresome it is
This beast that turns in my grave
Shrieking to unearth
Such fearful foreboding
Of what is to come
From what has been done
In the name of the Rose
That holds itself in
Enshrouded by sepals
To keep all its petals
From falling to ground
Out of sight, far from sound
Stalled in the bud
Distilled in the mud
Defended by prickle
Refusing to tickle
But piercing instead
The heart that yearns
To get out of bed

How exciting it is
This creature that rises with the sun
Singing its heart out
In radiant flower
Bearing fruit into joys to come
From what has been done
Crying, hip, hip hooray!
In the name of the Rose
That gathers all in
As it dies and grows
Loosing its petals
From the confines of sepals
To spread light in sound
Before turning back inward
Whilst falling to ground
Where others come to bear its energy away
Through death and decay
Into life that unfurls
In the opening
That sustains the possibility
Of flowering afresh
Through darkness in light
Breaking out of bounds
In another day

What is a Tree?

The tree which moves some to tears of joy is in the eyes of others
only a green thing which stands in the way. Some see nature as all
ridicule and deformity...and some scarce see nature at all. But by
the eyes of a man of imagination, nature is imagination itself
– William Blake

If we approach a tree as if it is little more than a solitary figure, a stake in the ground, set in a fixed reference frame by our objective eyesight, we may overlook its dynamic, living, context-dependent nature and consider its place in the world only as a potential resource, danger or obstacle to ourselves. Having no empathic feeling for how its past heritage and future potential are dynamically embodied in its present appearance as a manifestation of its habitat, any efforts that we make to manage its growth to suit our human desires may prove inadequate if not downright damaging to organism and environment alike.

If, on the other hand, we approach a tree seeking to understand it in ecological and evolutionary context from inside-out and from outside-in as a dynamic figure that both takes in and returns energy from and to its environmental ground, a more discerning relationship with its natural cycles of growth, death and decay may become possible. Instead of regarding the tree as an object, set in unnatural juxtaposition with and opposition to its natural neighbourhood, we understand it as a flow-form, like a river that simultaneously shapes and is shaped by the landscape it gathers and discharges from.

What is a Fungus?

> *a sickly autumn shone upon the land. Wet and rotten leaves reeked and festered under the foul haze. The fields were spotted with monstrous fungi of a size and colour never matched before – scarlet and mauve and liver and black – it was as though the sick earth had burst into foul pustules. Mildew and lichen mottled the walls and with that filthy crop, death sprang from the water-soaked earth*
> – Sir Arthur Conan Doyle

As with trees, it is all too easy to allow objective vision to take a one-sided view of fungi, which alienates them from their natural neighbourhood. But for fungi this view can all too readily miscast them in the mould of execrable underclass, the destroyers and takers of life. Attention then focuses selectively on how to prevent or remove their appearance, instead of appreciating their significance as the natural world's great communicators and recyclers, whose role in life's endings is vital to life's openings.

If, on the other hand, we come to view fungi as relay channels for energy flow between underworld and outer-world, a much deeper understanding of their role in natural processes of growth, death and decomposition may be possible. Instead of estranging them as some class of lowlife that subsists at the expense or, at best, by courtesy of the trickle down economy of the grandiose, we understand them as riverine channels, veins and arteries delivering and returning lifeblood through the body to and from the hearts of natural ecosystems.

By perceiving the flow-forms of fungi in this way, as energetic configurations of figure in ground and ground in figure that connect within, to and from those energetic configurations of figure in ground and ground in figure that comprise the flow-forms of trees, we may be better placed to question their role in the health and disease of those they include within their natural neighbourhood.

A Question of Health and Disease: How Do Trees and Fungi Relate?

From the foregoing, it is clear that we can address and hence answer this question in different ways. The answer that predominates, to this day, under the influence of positivist science and Darwinian evolutionary theory is 'as self-centred objects'. This is the answer that comes from our *rationalistic* predilection to impose definitive limits between subjects and objects as independent figures of 'one thing or another', regardless of the common ground of receptive space that both include and are included by as dynamic flow-forms. It is the answer that comes from dividing nature between 'one' as a 'whole' and 'many' as 'parts', and so sees life as a competition or 'power struggle' for 'superiority' over 'others'. But deep in the heart of this division lies profound inconsistency and paradox, rooted most fundamentally in the groundless supposition that material 'form' can be isolated from the immaterial 'space' that gives it size and shape. With this supposition comes an attitude of mind predisposed to conflict by making an enemy of 'other', out of the context of the limitless openness that pools all dynamically together as flow-form. And so it can be that fungi become represented either as 'foes', *against trees*, or as 'friends', *with trees* in their relentless struggle for life regardless of circumstances. At best, this representation is simplistic – the product of a crude mental removal of what is vital to life, which sacrifices 'truth' for the sake of 'convenience'. At worst it leads to abusive mismanagement and damage.

The answer seldom heard – as yet – comes from the *natural inclusional* understanding of energy flow as the dynamic inclusion of infinite receptive space in local form and local form in infinite space. According to this understanding, trees and fungi relate as natural neighbourhoods, with each as a dynamic inclusion of the other's influence. This understanding which also applies to all other life forms, including people, transforms the competitive representation of evolutionary processes on the basis of selective advantage, into a *co-creative* flow of all through all in receptive spatial context – the flow of *natural inclusion*.

'Fountains of the Forest' (Oil painting on board, by Alan Rayner, 1998).

"A tree is a solar powered fountain, its sprays supplied through wood-lined conduits and sealed in by bark until their final outburst in leaves...Within and upon its branching, enfolding, water-containing surfaces, and reaching out from there into air and soil are branching, enfolding, water-containing surfaces of finer scale, the mycelial networks of fungi...which provide a communications interface for energy transfer from neighbour to neighbour, from living to dead, and from dead to living" – Alan Rayner, Presidential Address, British Mycological Society, December 1998

Return from Calculus
To differentiate is not to define!
They put the cart before the horse
So that the poor thing got stuck in a rut
Those argumentative back-projectors
Newton and Leibniz
Whose deepest desire
Was to come first

Like Adam before Eve
On the Eve of their Fall

By cutting out space
From within the curve
Leaving the line shattered
Into helpless nonentities
Disguised as identities
By imposing minds

So that to integrate
We need only to add
What they failed to subtract
In their infinite regression
From All down to nought
But not quite

That informing presence
Adrift in our Time
Male without female
A self-negating false positive
With nowhere to hide
That takes us along
For its forgetful ride

Until some One gives notice
He can no longer bear
His harsh isolation
From somewhere to care

And rejoins his partner
In joyful communion
An affair of the heart
Where absence makes fonder

After millennia apart

And in that reunion
We need hardly add
What should never have been put asunder
By defining what's bad

A place that's beneath us
As we soar to great heights
Before returning the home
Subtracted from substance
To make solid figures
Meaningless in the absence
Of what needs them to care
For the receptive silence
Of everywhere

No, differentiation isn't what's wanted
To look askance
But it is what's needed
To configure variety
In complex self-dance
Of one within other
Transfigured by chance

Everywhere needs somewhere to love

Momentary Clarity
A clarity of recall
In the sound of waterfall
A silence within droplets
That hang upon the sword
Of edgy clamour

On its way to rest
Amongst upright rush
And horizontal lily
With never a cross word
To disturb their repose
In pooled togetherness
Of reflective communion

Instilling peace without time
Pressing upon the spirit
Of one phase in each other
Creating a third note
With a fifth and infinite dimension
Repairing the damage
Of two-faced deception
In that bipolar declaration
Of disorder in community

Here, amongst the gossiping tulip trees
Who swear allegiance
To one word or another
Enabling conflict to bespoken
Over the music of their tears

Now, let's dance in joyful rhythm
An eightsome reel
Of two resurrected to the power of three
Where one is a passage from nowhere

Not an idle momentum
Of dead point certainty
In monumental disregard
Concerning all that flows
Within and throughout

This vibrant tranquillity

Belonging only to a Life
That recalls with clarity
The all through one
And one for all
In corresponding triplicate
Without exception
Or deception

Channel Number Five
Come on you Two
Won't you fuse with us Three
So that we no longer have to be
Rivals?

In an Olympic Golden Sovereignty
Of One on either side of offence
That makes you over
Into binary opposition
An oddly singular couple
Of thrust and counter-thrust
In action and reaction
That denies the even handedness
Of your giving and taking
To and from each
Receptive and responsive influence

A tidal flow that empties
As it fills and fills
As it empties
In a chord with circumstantial need
To keep a breast

In tune with Mother
Who can give
No more than she can provide
If she is to sustain her sustaining
Identity of one in All and all in One
A world with out end
In which none can begin
Without being taken in
Amend

'**Channel No. 5'** (Oil painting on canvas by Alan Rayner, 2007).

From Vertex to Vortex and Beyond – Transfiguring The Geometry of Conflict

Walk tall, walk straight and look the world right in the eye, that's what my mama told me, when I was about knee high
– Val Doonican

Hello Darkness My Old Friend…a neon light that split the night and touched the sound of Silence
– Simon and Garfunkel

Pride after the Fall

We human beings are inclined to be very proud of our upright stance. We picture the evolutionary 'Ascent of Man' from a crawling past.

With this ascent came the possibility to use our hands far more manipulatively whilst focusing our powerful binocular eyesight and brains on catching and grasping whatever source of food or purchase or utility came our way. The resulting rewards of a combined sense of freedom to do as we please and security in having control over our destiny provide a source of exultation to this day. But there is also a hidden potential cost that few of us currently seem to recognize, let alone look straight in the eye, a cost to nothing less than our souls. For this ascent also set us up for the literal *orthodoxy* of a subjective-objective, rationalistic worldview in which our upright 'I' self confronts its surroundings as an adversary, perceiving life as a to-be-or-not-to-be 'struggle for existence'. It set the scene for us to view whatever is outside our bodily selves as being opposed to what is within ourselves – to make an 'enemy' of 'other' and in that process literally lose sight and feeling for our natural origins and neighbourhood. It is a powerful source of alienation from the Earthy substance beneath our feet and the other creatures that wander upon and within and over its surface. It lifts our heads above our hearts, reaching intellectually skywards, longing for yet further ascent to boost the sense of superiority of 'spirit-mind' over 'soulful body'. We begin to worship whatever is above and/or elevates us as 'positive' and to deplore whatever is beneath and/or lowers us as 'negative'. Caught somewhere in the cross-fire between the Heavens Above and the Underworld Below are our vulnerable Earthly selves, whose substantial 'growth' we celebrate and whose 'passing on' – whether of bodily 'waste' or 'life itself' – we recoil from.

Holding ourselves erect, in a posture of intrinsically unstable equilibrium, requires enormous effort and an incredible balancing act – as is all too evident from how tired we can get when wandering slowly around a museum or art gallery. What we really do seem to struggle against in this elevated position is the gravitational influence that continually draws us to Earth.

Perhaps this is what leads us mentally so readily to oppose 'vertical' to 'horizontal' and to represent this opposition in the fixed three-dimensional 'box' geometry of Euclid that has been enshrined as 'Sacred' to our culture. Everywhere, we plot 'progress' in graphical charts of *vertical against horizontal*, where 'ascent' means 'more' and 'descent' means 'less'.

But what, actually, do 'more' and 'less' mean in these representations? How do we *quantify* 'more' and 'less'? Is there anything we are forced to leave out of consideration in arriving at these quantities? And how might what we leave out actually be vital to the dynamic possibilities of life and soul?

This is where a very profound paradox and source of both internal and external conflict can enter our lives and psyches. In order to make quantitative comparisons between 'more' and 'less', we have to define exactly what we mean by these concepts both in terms of *what can be counted* and in terms of *what can't be counted*. And in seeking this definitive hard edge, we attempt the impossible, to edge out 'space' from 'matter' so that only material structure can be quantified – all else is set aside as 'immaterial'. Space is correspondingly either taken to amount to nothing at all or is made co-extensive with the structure of a rigid frame or surface. Instead of recognizing that space, as a presence of material absence or 'openness', is limitless, indivisible and uncontainable and hence infinite and non-localizable at all structural scales, we seek to divide it up into discrete units of distance or exclude it from consideration altogether as outside the boundary limits of *whole objects*. In mathematical terms, these objects comprise discrete numerical or geometrical *figures* and their internal subdivisions or fractions. The central character amongst these figures, which is taken both to incorporate and be a member of all of them, is a singular entity called 'One'.

'One', in conventional number theory, is a very strange and paradoxical figure indeed, because, *by definition*, it cannot incorporate whatever lies outside its boundary limit and so is consigned forever to stand alone as an absolute, independent singleness or 'Whole'. One is one and all alone and ever more shall be so; it truly is the loneliest number in the World! It is a number with no neighbourhood and hence no ground to stand on or be included within. No matter how many times you multiply one by itself all you get is the same as you started with. This is why 'two' is actually *not* the same as two separate ones. Two is a *couple* of *interdependent* ones, that is, two ones *pooled together in space*, which if multiplied by itself produces more than it was initially. This oddity of abstract mathematical formulation implicitly supports the 'holistic' notion of *emergence*, whereby the 'whole' is not the same as the 'sum' of its 'parts', and has found much recent application in non-linear dynamical systems models of evolutionary processes.

What kind of presence can a number with no neighbourhood have in Nature? The answer is startling for all those who may have taken its existence for granted for millennia and used it as the basis for precise measurements and calculations. It can have no *real* presence at all, other than as a figment of the imagination! Despite the vertical stature that we assign to it in the form of '1', it can actually amount to nothing more than a dimensionless point – the very same point, ironically, which is the paradoxical starting or end point of a 'line' in the conventional fixed Euclidean and non-Euclidean geometries of three-dimensional boxes and curved surfaces respectively.

Yet this is the very same kind of presence that we have come to associate with the singular identity of an individual 'I' self. It makes no sense because it has had removed from itself the very dimensionality of space that enables it to have a living presence in continuous dynamic communion with everywhere around that includes itself. In being definable as a singular, countable entity, it excludes what can neither be counted up nor down to – the 'zero' and 'infinity' of unaccounted-for space. It has lost the inextricable quality that makes it energetically alive and so become a dead still point in the wilderness of its own desolation. It has lost the *receptive* and *breathing* qualities of what might be called its 'soul' in the process of defining itself by standing up in opposition to its neighbourhood.

How, then, might this 'One' that is also called 'I' be rescued from its State of non-existence in opposition to other's existence that is called 'Independence'? The only possibility is by restoring the indefinable space that was banished from its purely material, frozen form in order to impose definition upon itself and other as discrete subject and object. No sooner is this restoration made, than the figure ceases to experience itself as a pure 'spirit-mind', a humility-lacking, living contradiction that seeks intellectual stature at the expense of emotional depth. Instead of viewing the world from the voyeuristic objective standpoint of an excluded observer, which judges the movement of all else against the fixed location of its own self-centre, it can now recognize itself as a dynamic inclusion of all it looks out on as a local expression of its non-local neighbourhood. The prospect opens for it to fulfil its creative potential as a soulfully embodied spirit with heart and mind relaxed in mutual support, not stiffened into conflict. In losing its absolute, simplistic self-definition, its true, complex self-identity is revealed as a dynamic local configuration of space, a *distinct* place *somewhere* as an inclusion of *everywhere*, not a *discrete*, independent singleness. Its body is no longer accountable for as a precisely quantifiable object or 'statistic', but becomes *somebody*, with a cavity at heart and infinity beyond, a natural local-in-non-local inclusion of the energy flow of the cosmos.

From Vertical against Horizontal to Tangential within Radial –
Melting into the Open Space Geometry of Natural Energy Flow
As soon as the Copernican Revolution revealed that the Earth's surface is not only curved, but also does not incorporate the single, fixed Centre of the Universe, it might also have been apparent that the same applies to the number 'One' and 'I' self. Orientations that *appear* to be vertical and horizontal to us as we stand with our feet on the ground and head in the air are, in reality, *radial* and *tangential* to the focal point of the Earth's local-in-non-local centre of gravity. Indeed, all straight lines and planes are *derivatives* from, not *precursors* of, a primarily non-linear geometry of dynamic flow-form as a local-in-non-local configuration of space, of which the simplest case – in which the ratio of surface area to *internal* volume [external volume being limitless] is minimal – is spherical. Hence there is nowhere that is absolutely 'Above', nor anywhere that is absolutely 'Below' anywhere else in the cosmos. There is only dynamic relationship relative to the inner-outer concavity and convexity of curved surfaces.

With this understanding comes the recognition that nowhere in the cosmos that is not frozen or crystallized into permanent stasis can adequately be represented by a solid, fully definable, closed figure or 'system' with its own fixed point-centre of 'mass' or 'force'. Instead, every figure capable of flux can only sensibly be understood primarily as a 'local sphere of non-local influence' or 'dynamic locality' whose 'focal-point' centre of thermal and gravitational receptivity shifts around in dynamic relationship with its neighbourhood.

For the rigid self-centre or axis of a purely local and independent number 1 or 'I', we have the shifting focus of a complex identity that incorporates what is tangential to its receptive inner spatial core or 'eye' through the dynamically interfacing boundaries of its non-local neighbourhood and passes this back on out again. The paradoxically stilled circulation of a stand-alone vertex becomes the spiralling inflows and outflows of what is not just a vortex, with finite or purely local limits, but infinitely more than a vortex, whose influence extends from somewhere to everywhere and vice versa.

What we have here in mathematical terms is a new kind of figure, both numerically and geometrically, that can openly include and be included in the influence of other(s) and so is more akin to the dynamic reality of natural flow-form than the discontinuous entities of classical and modern mathematics. What we have in psychological and philosophical terms is an infinitely expanded, dynamic sense of 'self as neighbourhood and neighbourhood as self'.

This is truly a figure *trans*figured *through* its taking of the open space of 'other' to heart, dissolving the unnatural opposition between the 'light' of 'spirit-mind' and 'darkness' of 'soulful body' and bringing them into the natural, mutually inclusive communion of 'sound in silence'. Philosophically and scientifically, it corresponds with what has been called 'inclusionality', the understanding of natural energy flow as the dynamic inclusion of space in form and form in space. Mathematically it is the child of what has been called 'Transfigural Mathematics' by its founder, Lere Shakunle.

Far from being an active-reactive entity that does things to others and has things done to it by others, this figure is a complex identity with a receptive, reflective and responsive core. This core takes in and circulates as it empties out in continuous dynamic relationship with the flow of the natural neighbourhood that it both dynamically embodies and is embodied in. In the process it sustains a dynamic balance of *zero* between reciprocal inflows and outflows from and out into the infinite non-local space of everywhere, in much the same way that a mammalian heart sustains the balance between venous and arterial circulations via the breathing-place of the lungs.

This, then, is not a figure that banishes the zero and infinity of receptive open space to somewhere beyond its self-defining limits, but instead continuously incorporates these within its core identity and environmental neighbourhood. It is not a singular 'One' isolated between zero and two, but a one that includes zero at heart and two within its reach and from there every other numerical identity from 'plus' to 'minus' infinity. For this reason it has been called a 'zeroid' or *zero id*entity.

From Standing Start to Crawling Reach

So perhaps when we celebrate the 'Ascent of Man' from 'creepy-crawlies' it might be as well not to denigrate the latter as 'beneath us', but to recognize instead the vitality to the natural flow of life of including tangential reach within radial alignment. Perhaps if we were to meet with one another on 'all fours' we might even find in that tangential orientation of head alongside heart a position of greater natural humility and common spirit-edness, less liable to rear up into confrontational posture! Maybe a fundamental redesign of the geometry of our governmental institutions is called for if ever the possibility is to emerge of true democracy in which all are steered through all, within the flow of a river that can never be the same twice, as Heraclitus described thousands of years ago. Then we might return 'home', both intellectually and emotionally, to a place both within and beyond our local self-interest. A place which was always there before the objective rationality of Plato, Aristotle and their camp followers claimed hierarchical dominion for Man over Woman and Nature, and always will be here, wherever we search feelingly for it in the silent space of darkness dynamically configured by light.

What Happens Now?

So, what happens now?
In the space between my ears
Vacant in the yearning of the moment
Of a silence unheard
By a constant ticking

Positive affirmation
Of rectitude
That double crosses
By marking out
Where sanity begins

At the edge of nowhere
Included in somewhere
Forlorn in spirit
Dampened under cover
Of fire blankets

Without enthusiasm
How can passion fruit?
At the edge of somewhere
Included in everywhere
Beyond control
Of ardent striving

Arrested at rest
In helpless worrying
Beyond the call of duty
That forbids
Forbidding silence

Where are the words
To call to order

The mind that strays
Beyond its limits
In splendid isolation?

Cascading, overflowing
Across some edge
That tightens sinews
In tense anticipation
Of what's to come
When what's forbidden
Is bidden to some

Who cannot suppress
That tense outflowing
By getting a grip
On what's born to run

A gift that passes
Around and around
Until someone gets it
And all is undone

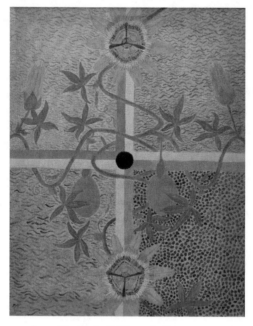

'How Compassion Fruits' (Oil painting on canvas, by Alan Rayner, 2008). *Life, love and suffering spring from the same source of receptive space that is present within, throughout and beyond the earth, air, fire and water of inspiring and expiring natural flow-forms as energetic configurations. These natural figures dynamically balance receptive negative influence and responsive positive influence through the reflective zero-point core of their local and non-local self-identity.*

From Juxtaposition to Reciprocal Flow – the Natural Inclusion of Figure in Ground and Ground in Figure

Rank and File – Figures in Fixed Alignment
It seems to be difficult for us, as we look out at what lies beyond the confines of our human skins, to avoid gaining the instantaneous impression that the world and Universe consist of independent objects set beside one another with varying distances of space between them. Whether they be trees, stars, birds, stones, soldiers or next-door neighbours, we see these

objects as material 'figures', both surrounded and isolated by the spatial 'ground' of their environmental surroundings.

This is the impression that has been built into the rationalistic logical and mathematical foundations upon which an enormous edifice of human thought has been constructed, which to this day affects almost every aspect of our theories and practice of science, art, theology, education and governance. In one way and another, it has distanced us from one another and our natural neighbourhood, unable to break through the self-installed barriers of what Darwin alluded to as a 'struggle for existence'. The perceived *discontinuities* transform what promises to be the most profound source of human love and creativity into the deepest pit of human conflict and waste. They lead us to try to dispel or confine the 'darkness' that permeates the heart and soul of every living body and put the purified 'light' of 'intellectual spirit' in its place. They force us to tear ourselves and our world asunder, whilst believing that in the process what we are 'doing' is somehow 'good' – with sound reason and evidence, if not 'God', on 'our side'. Nothing could be further from the truth, based as it is on a fundamental misunderstanding of natural energy flow and its dynamic local manifestations. If anything, through seeking the impossible purification of light from darkness, like gold from base metal, we sever ourselves from the 'God' of 'Nature herself', whilst doggedly persisting in the absolute belief that we can and do know the difference between what's best and what's worst, regardless of context.

Literally at the 'square root' of the severance of 'figures' from their natural neighbourhood is their paradoxical treatment as *discrete numbers and geometrical entities*, of which the most singular and central character is called 'One' and represented as an absolute unit of 'mass' or 'force' called a 'point'. The *oddest thing*, again quite literally, about this figure, is its complete isolation from its ground, which makes it an *exclusive whole* that can be no more and no less than *its self alone*. 'Other' numbers are regarded either as fractional 'parts' of this 'whole', or themselves to be 'wholes', that is as 'sets' or 'groups' of 'ones' added together – twosomes, threesomes, foursomes, etc, such that 'one' can be assembled from 'many' and many can be assembled into 'one'. The problem here is that as long as 'one' is 'all alone', it cannot be assembled from 'ones' that are also all alone, because these ones cannot include the space between themselves that would allow them to be together. This is evident from the fact that 'one' is the only number that, when multiplied by 'itself', that is, 'squared', yields exactly the same as it was before. Any 'fractional' number less than 'one' yields less than it was before when squared and any 'collective' number, such as 'two', yields more than it was before.

This oddity arises literally because 'somewhere along the line', 'space' is omitted from the definition of material 'quantity', such that each quantity is treated as a discrete 'individual' or 'collective' 'unit' with a *finite boundary limit*. Space is omitted both because it appears to consist of 'nothing', an 'immaterial' absence of material presence, and because to include it – as an indefinable, non-containable and hence *infinite* presence of material absence – would actually make absolute material definition and measurement of *finite* quantities impossible. In other words, space is omitted not for the sake of 'objective truth', as rationalistic thinkers might claim – for there can be no such thing as 'objective truth' in a world that is not absolutely definable – but for the sake of *convenience*. Along with the omission comes a false but addictive sense of freedom and security in having *dominion* over an ultimately knowable, predictable and controllable Nature, freed from the vicissitudes that weary and frighten the human spirit.

In reality, to ignore the space beyond a figure's boundary is to preclude any understanding of that figure's dynamic evolutionary relationship with others in its vicinity. This is why, at least in terms of conventional mathematics, Albert Einstein was right to recognize that:

As far as the laws of mathematics refer to reality, they are not certain, and as far as they are certain, they do not refer to reality

The human tragedy is that we continue to impose this abstract view of reality, with all its oppressive restrictions and incomprehension of what comes naturally, not only upon Nature herself but on our human selves that Nature inescapably includes and nurtures in her receptive womb. We rank and file ourselves as we rank and defile Nature, setting the scene for profound social, psychological and environmental distress even as we glorify in our apparent technological prowess. Everywhere, the one-dimensional line is drawn, with discrete numerical points set out like mileposts along it, between 'here' and 'there', 'me' and 'you', 'us' and 'them', 'success' and 'failure', 'winners' and 'losers', 'rich' and 'poor', 'first' and 'last', 'alive' and 'dead', 'ends' and 'means' – with little thought given to the dreadful costs incurred in the wastelands along its margins. Hardly anywhere is consideration given to the diversity of community and harmonious attunement needed to sustain life, love and learning in an ever-evolving scene with no fixed limits. Biological evolution itself is most commonly depicted as a 'rat race' for winners to take all and run like Red Queens on the spot to stay on their throne. All is sacrificed in the strife for hierarchical ascendancy, all for the sake of avoiding nothing, and in that avoidance, falling into the peculiar grief that comes when intellectual spirit declares war upon its soulful heart.

The Transfiguration of 'One Alone': Naturally Including the Dark Ground of Being in Becoming
Just as we might gain the impression of a world of juxtaposed objects in an instant, so it need not take long for us, for example when watching contemplatively from a riverbank, to recognize

that what can appear to be set apart in a frozen moment may in reality both be emerging from and entering into one another's flow. In that melting moment, the possibility arises for our understanding of the fundamental nature of 'One', and with it our understanding of our unique individual self-identities, to *transfigure*. The freeze-framed entity of 'one all alone' opens up receptively, reflectively and responsively to the natural neighbourhood of and in which it is a dynamic inclusion, a *flow-form* that energetically both gains from and contributes to its spatially limitless surroundings. Through that opening, passion, compassion and creativity enter our lives. For the inert, dimensionless, particulate 'point-masses' and 'point-forces' of rationalistic abstraction, we have the living, breathing, dimension-full 'point-influences' of natural energy flow in which no number can be without neighbourhood, and no neighbourhood can be defined absolutely. This is what William Wordsworth recognized, when his poetic imagination allowed him to comment:

> *In nature everything is distinct, yet nothing defined into absolute, independent singleness*

This is the natural reality recognized in the logical foundations of 'natural inclusionality' and *'transfigural mathematics'*, which extend radically beyond, whilst nonetheless offering the possibility of embracing and transforming what has been learned through objective rationality. Inclusionality is the understanding of natural energy flow as the dynamic inclusion of space in form and form in space. Literally meaning *'through or across*-figural mathematics', *trans*figural mathematics, founded by Lere Shakunle, treats both numerical and geometric 'figures' as open dynamic flow-forms *permeated* by space, not closed-off entities that either occupy or are confined by 'space' as a fixed three-dimensional framework or curved surface. Correspondingly, these figures cannot be abstracted from the spatial context that they both *fold into and in from*, and space is not a meaningless 'absence of presence' or 'emptiness', but instead a limitless, receptive presence of 'openness', full of *creative potential*.

It is important to appreciate that this kind of fluid understanding of natural form *only* becomes possible when *space*, as limitless openness, is acknowledged to be *omnipresent*. This means that there can be no cut-off or discontinuity between the space that surrounds and the space that permeates the dynamic boundaries of locally distinguishable form(s). A 'figure' is not just *surrounded* by its environmental 'ground', it *inextricably includes* the space that is continuous with its surroundings. It is neither possible to confine space within a bottle, nor to exclude space from the bottle. All that can be so confined or excluded – and even then not completely or permanently – is what dynamically embodies space in form, by way of certain intensities of what is currently called 'electromagnetic radiation', only some of which is visible to human eyes as 'light'.

In other words, *space* – not some abstract, locally situated, powerful material agency or 'force' – is the *real unmoved mover* of Nature. Space, being infinite, non-resistive and everywhere (non-local) can exceed local form ('somewhere'), but local form cannot exceed space. By the same token, space itself does not flow – it just *is*, here, there and everywhere as the Dark, Silent Ground of Being that is dynamically embodied in the Becoming of natural Flow-Form. *Form* flows as the dynamic local ['electromagnetic'] configuration of space in space, that is, as a 'figure' that dynamically includes – as distinct from excludes/opposes/juxtaposes (as per rationalism) – its 'ground' (the Dark, Silent Ground of Being).

The Vital Synergy of 'Positive' and 'Negative' Influences
It is as though space, in the presence of form, has a *receptive influence* or 'suction', to which form *responds* in a potentially enormous, but never completely unconstrained (i.e. 'random'),

variety of dynamic configurations. What has rationalistically been regarded either as the 'destructive negativity' or unaccountable, passive 'nothingness' of space is here seen as a co-creative quality, which far from 'subtracting' from closed, 'positive' form *transfigures* form into open, dynamic responsiveness. Instead of having 'positive figure' set against 'negative space', as is commonly described in art theory, for example, each dynamically includes the other in ongoing evolutionary flow, the one opening up, the other responsively embodying creative possibility.

Instead of a battle between the 'forces' of 'light' and 'darkness', 'positive' and 'negative', 'spirit' and 'soul' – with our mortal bodies caught in the fury of their cross-fire – life dances in their mutually inclusive interplay of Figure ('I') in Ground ('-') and Ground in Figure, a gift of natural energy flow that we can receive, protect and pass on . Its peace-filled story continues as an endless circulation of each within the other *ad infinitum*.

Infinity - + - + - Infinity

From Dialectics to Inclusionality – Transfiguring the 'Nucleus of Contradiction' Into the 'Nucleus of Reciprocity'
From a paper with Jack Whitehead

Summary
The last 2,500 years have seen an unresolved conflict between propositional and dialectical logicians. Here, whilst acknowledging the *partial* validity of their views, we trace the confrontation between these logicians to an unrealistic premise that both paradoxically share: the supposition that nature is completely definable into discrete, mutually exclusive categories of subject and object. This *exclusion of the middle ground* is deeply embedded in orthodox theories and practices of science, theology, education and governance as well as in our mathe-

matics and language. Whereas it leads propositional logicians, following Aristotle, to accept one statement about a perceived entity in reality as necessarily 'true' or 'present' and to reject the other as 'false' or 'absent', it leads dialectical thinkers to accept contradictory statements as the nucleus of an inherently ambiguous and pluralistic Nature.

Inclusionality is an understanding of all natural form as 'flow-form' – an energetic configuration of space in figure and figure in space. The inherently static logic of mutual exclusion is thereby subsumed by a fluid logic of 'the including middle', where the latter is the seat of dynamic correspondence, not dichotomy, between local informational and non-local spatial presences. These presences combine in dynamically distinct but not isolated bodily identities as natural inclusions of 'everywhere' in 'somewhere'.

This understanding hence offers a way of including within a 'nucleus of reciprocity', i.e. *the reciprocal influence of each in the other*, what is rejected by propositional logicians as 'not present' but accepted by dialectical thinkers as 'contradictory'. At its root is the simple acknowledgement of space as a continuous, infinite depth throughout the cosmos, *which cannot be cut and so does not stop at boundaries.* No dynamic organization or boundary can, in reality, be absolutely closed.

Space, Boundaries and the Fixed Roots of Conflicting Logic
Propositional thinkers can reject dialectical claims to knowledge as, *'without the slightest foundation. Indeed, they are based on nothing better than a loose and woolly way of speaking'* (Popper 1963, p. 316). Dialectical thinkers claim that propositional thinking masks the dialectical nature of reality (Marcuse, 1964).

How is it that such uncompromisingly opposed views of reality could have been held – and continue to be held – with such faith in their validity by their proponents throughout 2,500 years of the history of human thought? Could both be valid in their own way? Is there a way in which they could be reconciled, and what would such reconciliation imply for our understanding of nature and human nature? Would such reconciliation necessitate the development of a new system of logic that transcends or transfigures both? These are the questions we intend to address in this paper.

We begin by acknowledging the influence that perceptions of space and boundaries have upon the way we think about natural form and processes. As terrestrial, bipedal, omnivorous primates with binocular vision, huge frontal brain hemispheres and opposable thumbs that equip us to discriminate between and grasp whatever we need to feed, protect and make our way in the world, we are great natural categorizers. It comes easily to us to discriminate between visible, tangible 'things' and the apparent 'gaps' or 'discontinuities' of 'empty space' that appear to come between them.

Correspondingly, it is very easy for us to develop a hard-line logic of discontinuity between 'something' and 'nothing', to reinforce this in our language and mathematics, and thence to embed it deep in the foundations of our theories and practices of science, theology, education and governance. We come to assume that every distinguishable form must have a boundary limit where it stops and something or somewhere else begins. By the same token, we are forced to assume that everything must originate from some kind of 'start point' and either continue indefinitely or disappear into some 'end point'.

Convenient, communicable and incontrovertible as the resultant hard-line separation and quantification of material objects from their spatial context may appear to be, it is the source of profound paradox and conflict – including that which obtains between propositional and dialectic thinkers. A moment's insight reveals its inherent inconsistency. If natural form was purely material, it could consist of no more than a dimensionless point with no shape or size. If natural form was purely spatial, it would be featureless. If nature consisted purely of solid, massy particles and space wasn't a natural presence, nothing could move. If space was just an infinite emptiness surrounding discrete objects, there would be no place to situate an external source of force to move these objects around. If space wasn't within and throughout as well as around natural form, it wouldn't be possible for form to be distinguishable or to flow as liquid or gas or to have variable qualities of density, bounciness, flexibility and conductivity.

Inclusionality – Natural Energy Flow as the Dynamic Inclusion of Space in Form and Form in Space

The inescapable conclusion is that the natural world of movement and mobility that we sense and inhabit cannot be defined completely into hard and fast categories. There is no absolutely closed form that we know of or can know of. Space is dynamically included in form and form in space. Space is an indivisible, indefinable presence of openness everywhere, infinite at all scales, not an empty absence of definable presence within or outside the finite bounds of discrete, active and reactive material objects. In relationship with dynamical form, space has a receptive quality that *induces* flow. In relationship with omnipresent space, dynamical form has a responsive quality that enables it to flow into place. Within this place, receptive space and responsive form combine reflectively and protectively to co-create a dynamic, local-in-non-local 'nucleus of reciprocity' of each within the reciprocal influence of the other. This nucleus comprises the 'inner core' or 'bodily' identity of a natural 'flow-form', which is locally distinct but spatially and dynamically continuous with the 'outer environment' or 'natural neighbourhood' that it both feeds from and feeds into as an inclusion of an endless circulation. In other words, this nucleus comprises what might be called a 'breathing point', fundamentally different from the abstract, dimensionless, purely local points of rationalistic logic and mathematics. Indeed, it corresponds with what has been called the 'zeroid' or 'zero identity' by the founder of 'Transfigural Mathematics', Lere Shakunle.

This is the understanding of the evolutionary essence of natural energy flow that has been called 'inclusionality', to distinguish it from the objective rationality that underpins both propositional and dialectic thinking. It accords with the *trans-figural* mathematical logic, first developed by Shakunle in 1985, in that flow occurs *through* naturally *continuous* numerical and geometrical figures as dynamic local-in-non-local embodiments of space, *not* as the result of enforced movement of discontinuous figures *through space*.

'I-opening': the Inclusional 'Self' in Life, Love and Learning
The implications of this natural understanding for the way we view our human place in nature are enormous. They represent a radical upheaval in the logic that we have been teaching ourselves to accept without question for millennia. From this rationalistic logic, which enforces propositional thinkers to regard 'self' as 'autonomous' and dialectic thinkers to regard it as a nucleus of 'living contradiction' (Ilyenkov, 1977), we arrive into the natural logic of inclusionality that enables us to regard self as 'living neighbourhood', a 'nucleus of reciprocity' or *reciprocal influence of each in the other*.

In the case of human beings, a 'self' that is aware of its inclusional nature approaches life with a very different *attitude* from the 'imperious one' that holds itself apart from all else as an independent entity. Unlike the latter, this inclusional self' doesn't confront its environmental surroundings or 'wild side' as a contestant that must be subjugated and exploited in order to sustain order and survive. Indeed, the very nature of its 'self-interest' expands from 'one' that excludes or contradicts 'other', to one that dynamically includes other in itself and itself in other. It correspondingly views its dynamic bodily locality as a fluid inclusion of all it beholds, not as a voyeuristic excluded observer peering out at an 'objective world out there' as if through a window in its soul. It feels the space in its heart that makes room for the inclusion of others, just as others make room for its flow to enter their hearts. This gives rise to the feeling called *empathy*, which associates with love and compassion.

This inclusional self is expressed in the world with the pride of humility that finds pleasure in learning and work well done, not the Pride of arrogance that claims sovereign superiority over others. It does not seek to compete, though it may well compare its competence with others in its neighbourhood as a healthy way of identifying possibilities for enhancement and creative innovation. It recognizes its vulnerability, along with others', not as 'weakness' or 'failure' but as vital to the possibility of living, learning and passing on co-creatively in its continually-evolving neighbourhood of natural energy flow.

The Inclusional Self in Practice – The Mind-and-Soul-Full Educator of Self and Other

So what does the inclusional self look like in practice? Does it have an inclusional practice, a way of behaving, which can be learned? What kind of theory might underlie this practice?

From what we have already said, it is clear that inclusional ways of living, loving and learning emerge from an attitude of mind and heart, not from following a set procedure or boning up on written texts whose words cannot in themselves convey the depths of feeling and intuition involved. This attitude is intellectually justifiable in terms of an understanding of natural energy flow as the dynamic inclusion of space in form and form in space, which contrasts with the fixed, definable form assumed by objective rationality to be the primary, default condition of Nature.

But this doesn't mean inclusionality can only be practiced by an elite class of people with esoteric knowledge and understanding. Indeed, if anything inclusional behaviour comes most naturally to anyone whose attitude has not been restricted by the exclusive theories and practices that we have been teaching ourselves for millennia.

Inclusional ways of relating are correspondingly most evident when we feel relaxed in surroundings and company that we love – especially beyond the confines of what many of us regard as our *workplace*. And therein may lie a lesson in itself – that we experience most difficulty in living a life of 'self as neighbourhood' in settings that we have come to associate with *work*. For it is just for such settings that we have used fixed assumptions of objective rationality to *entrain* and control ourselves as unthinking robotic followers of instruction in restrictive practices – not *educate* us into a wider awareness of our human creative potential.

It is as though we regard work not as a source of mutual sustenance and pleasure, but rather as a stern obligation of what we must do to survive in the harsh reality of life as a battleground, not the adventure of life as a playground. This is most painfully obvious when the workplace really *is* a battleground. Here is how John Keegan (2004) describes military training:

> ...the deliberate injection of emotion...will seriously hinder, if not altogether defeat, the aim of officer-training. That aim...is to reduce the conduct of war to a set of rules and a system of procedures – and thereby make orderly and rational what is essentially chaotic and instinctive. It is an aim analogous to that pursued by medical schools in their fostering among students of a detached attitude to pain and distress... the rote-learning and repetitive form and the categorical, reductive quality ...has an important and intended psychological effect. Anti-militarists would call it depersonalizing and even dehumanizing. But given...that battles are going to happen, it is powerfully beneficial...one is helping him to avert the onset

of fear, or, worse, of panic...

Here it is all too clear how the assumption that conflict is inevitable becomes a self-fulfilling prophecy, which rationalistically objectifies the person by excising or confining the limitless space that brings uncertainty and vulnerability (and love) and imposes in its place a rigid frame of deadening predictability. The 'self' is sustained in a confrontational stance as an automaton or living contradiction of its natural neighbourhood through mindless and heartless routine and ritual, in which learning is reduced to rehearsal for one kind of prescriptively-staged performance or another. Sense, sensibility and creativity are ruled out by rules and regulations of pride, prejudice and habit that define what can and what cannot be accepted by the *status quo*.

The resultant addictive patterns of thought and behaviour subservient to prescriptive codes of conduct and practice are evident throughout modern human culture in the hierarchical and adversarial design of our academic, governmental, industrial, commercial, religious and sporting organizations. Everywhere, this design impedes evolutionary possibility through the imposition of megalithic structures that oppose change. It even projects itself on to instead of learning from the energy flow of non-human nature, exemplified by the Darwinian oxymoron of 'natural selection' as the 'preservation of favoured races in the struggle for life'.

Such thinking cannot, by its very nature, solve the enormous environmental, social and psychological problems of its own making that humanity sees as confronting itself at the beginning of the twenty-first century. It is its own worst enemy.

This is where the inclusional way of thinking about 'self' could help greatly. It becomes possible not to regard 'self' as a 'fixed locality', stuck forever in the same old skin, with the same old genes controlling its every move, on course for inevitable competition and conflict. Instead self is understandable as a dynamic locality of its non-local natural neighbourhood, capable both of changing and being changed by its circumstances, like a river in landscape that is never the same twice. This is essentially how inclusionality provides the kind of 'unhooked thinking' that can help us out of the helplessness (often 'learned' and culturally enforced) of assuming addictive behaviour is pre-ordained – a 'problem with us' as singular individuals, as distinct from 'a problem for us' as 'living neighbourhoods'. And in getting ourselves 'off the hook' it may be possible to unleash enormous creative potential that is inherent in our capacity for 'play'. Instead of instructing ourselves to conform to pre-selective standards, we truly educate ourselves to become involved in an ongoing, improvisational process of 'natural inclusion' – the fluid dynamic, co-creative transformation of all through all in receptive spatial context.

From 'Space-Time' to 'Place-Time': The evolutionary geometry of natural inclusion

Have you ever found yourself in 'the wrong place at the wrong time'? For that matter, have you ever found yourself in the 'right place at the right time'? Such is the nature of our human experience of misadventure and serendipity – experience that if we are honest with ourselves informs us all too clearly about how context-dependent our seeming successes and failures are, and how inapt it is either to assume *sole* credit or deny *any* responsibility for them.

Who we are and how we fare depends on *where* we find ourselves, and where we find ourselves cannot be isolated from the space that both includes and is included by the dynamic configurations of our bodily boundaries. We are always *somewhere* locally unique as dynamic inclusions of a boundless, non-local everywhere. We are continually in transition, inhabitants of a dynamic neighbourhood of ever-transforming spatial relationship that simultaneously both shapes and is shaped by us, like the water in a river that both creates and follows paths of least resistance to its flow.

We cannot, therefore, make random exceptions of ourselves from Nature, as if we were independently definable objects, capable of being anywhere, anytime and driven hither and thither from some magical, forceful control centre somewhere either outside or inside the fixed definition of our bodies and living space. But that is precisely what rationalistic logic, based ultimately on the exclusion of 'space' as 'void nothing' from 'matter' as 'definite something', has been persuading us to try vainly to 'do' for millennia, whilst becoming ever more deeply entrenched in our philosophical, mathematical and scientific foundations. The fundamental premise of this logic – the existence of independently definable and quantifiable objects – lies in an idealized freezing out of 'imperfection' (i.e. 'space') from discrete and regularized geometrical form, constrained within a three-dimensional box extended to infinity.

This abstract imposition of discontinuity by definition neither takes account of nor does justice to contemporary scientific findings and real life experience of the dynamic continuity of natural flow. Yet it continues to be defended most zealously by those whose claim to authority rests in what they regard as disinterested objective observation and evidence. It also leads to the deep paradox, conflict, waste and damage that arises through dislocating 'self' from 'neighbourhood', making us believe in an unsustainable, competitive struggle for existence and individual perfection that is at odds with the variability of the natural world that both sustains and includes us.

The scientific beginnings of the ending of this dislocation, and associated recovery in awareness of our dynamically-continuous natural geometry, have emerged with the advent of relativity, quantum mechanics and non-linear dynamical systems theory. All these theories signify, in one way or another, the inextricability of space from matter in a fluid dynamic cosmos of energy flow.

None of these theories, however, has yet been able to escape from self-imposed logical and mathematical constraints based on definitive initial assumptions, an upshot of which is that what is implicitly complementary in their reciprocal views of spatial inclusion in natural geometry appears to be contradictory. In particular, there has been continual altercation amongst proponents of 'stochastic' and 'deterministic' interpretations of dynamic processes. The former interpretations are based on models that default to a random distribution of independent events or objects, arising in effect from the degenerative influence of space, which results in an inexorable rise in 'entropy' ('disorder') within a defined system. The latter assume that all future evolution of a system is fully dependent upon (i.e. 'fixed' or 'fated' by) 'initial conditions'. These conditions are defined within a local frame or 'attractor' of space at an instant beginning point in time, albeit that tiny differences in these conditions can be amplified into enormous changes in long-term behaviour (the famous 'butterfly effect' of chaos theory).

The altercation between deterministic and stochastic views of evolutionary processes is epitomized by the inconsistency between Einstein's saying on the one hand that the environment is 'everything except me' and on the other his protestation against quantum theory that 'God does not play dice'. The origin of this altercation lies in the alternative fixed geometries of space within which the two views are framed, neither of which is supported by actual evidence or experience. In these geometries space is either confined, along with time, to the curved surface of a zero-thickness fabric that gets locally warped by material condensations of energy, or within a rigid container that discrete objects can pop into or out of , as if from or into nothing or nowhere.

This altercation parallels the 2,500 year-old battle between propositional ('either/or') and dialectical ('both/and in mutual contradiction'), and associated reductive and holistic forms of logic, each of which assumes the independent existence of definable *whole* entities whilst rejecting the rationality of the other's position. The battle, along with its implications for the origins of human conflict, is eloquently depicted in the following excerpt from C.S. Lewis's 'Screwtape Letters' from a senior to an apprentice devil:

The whole philosophy of Hell rests on a recognition of the axiom that one thing is not another thing, and, specifically, that one self is not another self. My good is my good and your good is yours. What one gains another loses. Even an inanimate object is what it is by excluding all other objects from the space it occupies; as it expands, it does so by pushing all other objects aside or by absorbing them. A self does the same. With beasts the absorption takes the form of eating; for us, it means the sucking of will and freedom out of a weaker self into a stronger. 'To be' means 'to be in competition'. Now the Enemy's philosophy is nothing more or less than one continued attempt to evade this very obvious truth. He aims at contradiction. Things are to be many, yet also one. The good of one self is to be the good of another. This impossibility He calls love, and this same monotonous panacea can be detected under all He does and even all He is – or claims to be. Thus He is not content, even Himself, to be a sheer arithmetical unity; He claims to be three as well as one, in order that this nonsense about Love may find a foothold in his own nature. At the other end of the scale, He intro-duces into matter that obscene invention the organism, in which the parts are perverted from their natural destiny of competition and made to cooperate...
Family... is like the organism, only worse; for the members of the family are distinct, yet also united in a more conscious and respon-sible way. The whole thing, in fact, turns out to be simply one more device for dragging in Love.

No sooner are the restrictive definitions of matter, space and time relaxed, however, than a fluid geometry of Nature becomes obvious, in which local figure, as a concentration of energy, is understood to be a responsive dynamic inclusion of receptive immaterial space and vice versa. The figural and spatial phases are as solute and solvent are to one another in a natural solution, and the fluid geometry is to the fixed geometry as water is to ice, not in opposition to one another but in mutually-transforming dynamic relationship. The receptive ('loving') influence of space extends everywhere without having to be dragged into paradoxically defined subjects and objects.

The concepts of 'inclusionality' and 'natural inclusion' that arise from appreciation of this fluid geometry offer a new logical foundation for understanding the dynamic relational quality of living systems in a more realistic and contextually aware way, which transcends the definitive limitations of propositional and dialectic formulations. Correspondingly, inclusionality can be described, but not defined, as a comprehension of Nature as a fluid continuum of mutually inclusive local figural and non-local spatial phases in which all form is flow-form, a dynamic receptive-responsive configuration of everywhere in somewhere, with no fixed centre. Natural inclusion is the co-creative, fluid dynamic transformation of all through all in receptive spatial context.

With these concepts, matter and space mutually melt into a heterogeneous, variable viscosity energy flow of 'place-time' or 'co-creative evolutionary geometry'. Notions of both 'competition' and 'co-operation' are understood to be predicated upon the prescriptive definition of at least initially discrete entities, for which there is no evidence and which does not make sense of actual scientific observations or personal experience of natural dynamic communion. Similarly, notions of 'selfishness' and 'altruism', based on the definitive assertion or denial of self-centredness are subsumed by awareness that our complex local-non-local self-identity arises within the dynamic context of, not in isolation from natural neighbourhood, and varies accordingly. To understand ourselves and others we ask not 'who' or 'what' we are as objects occupying the fabric of space-time, but 'where' we are as dynamic inclusions of the continuum of place-time. The whole basis for the philosophy of Hell collapses and Love, as receptive-responsive influence, is a dynamic inclusion of all, without contradiction.

The Exclusional and Inclusional Making of Circles and Spheres

Nothing could be more natural than circular and spherical form. We encounter such forms, along with their spiral, elliptical and tubular progeny, everywhere in the natural world, from sub-atomic to galactic scales. But when we come to reflect on the origin and relationships of these forms, we encounter a very profound problem. This problem is, quite simply, that the way circular form arises naturally is the inverse of the way it is conventionally treated mathematically. In a nutshell, whereas natural circular form primarily arises inwardly, that is via energy flow from everywhere around into a dynamic receptive centre or focal space, like that at the eye of a hurricane or within a bubble, conventional mathematical form is constructed outwardly from a fixed central control point. In other words, natural form arises as a dynamic relational *hole*, balancing energy inflows and outflows via informational interfacing between inner worlds and outer worlds that are distinguishable but not isolatable from one another. By contrast, conventional mathematical form arises as a *whole*, paradoxically isolated from its environmental context and so *completely* self-contained – as when a circle is constructed via the rotational transformation of a radial straight line using a set of compasses.

At the heart of this contrast is the dislocation of matter from space, which is embedded in the incorrigibly discontinuous foundations of classical and modern mathematics. With this dislocation, the possibility of including the inductive influence of receptive space in natural energy flow is lost, such that all representations of physical form and process are based on material information alone, externally or internally forced into action and reaction by some ineffable agency. Space is either excluded altogether or conflated with a definitive structural framework, whether this is the three-dimensional cube of Euclidian geometry, or the depthless curved surface of conventional non-Euclidian geometries.

As long as fixed mathematical form does not correspond with dynamic natural form, the use of mathematical models and arguments to explain, predict or indeed manage nature and human nature is liable to be misleading and damaging. So, the question arises as to what kind of mathematical foundations could more adequately represent natural form and processes.

To begin with, realistic mathematical foundations need to include space as an omnipresence, throughout nature, which can neither be excluded from nor conflated with fixed structure. Correspondingly, space is infinite and therefore immeasurable at any and every scale. Only pure, finite, material information would be quantifiable in discrete units – this being the basis for conventional mathematics – but since space and matter are naturally mutually inclusive as a continuous energy flow, no measurement can realistically be referred independently to a single scale. Comparisons made between 'greater' and 'lesser' forms, as if they are discrete objects inhabiting a 'level playing field', are therefore intrinsically *un*fair, because natural fluid dynamic geometry is heterogeneous, all-inclusive and many-scaled, not uniform. Every form is a marriage of local, finite energetic figure with non-local, infinite space, unique in its local situation but in communion with all others through the omnipresence of space, which both includes and is included by all. Infinity cannot be a singular, discrete entity with fixed location, nor indeed many discrete entities combined into one. Infinity is all space, which includes and comprises many spaces or 'relative infinities', which in turn comprise the habitats of locally unique flow-forms as 'somewhere including everywheres' nested over all scales from macrocosm to microcosm.

Here, it needs to be appreciated that space as an omnipresence would be formless in the absence of any figural content. It therefore makes no sense to talk about the influence or otherwise of space as an independent entity. This is why purely material-based explications of nature treat space paradoxically as a passive absence, which can conveniently be ignored, not an influential presence, which cannot. But no sooner are space and information understood to be distinct but mutually inclusive in natural energy flow, not independent or conflated, than the possibility emerges of recognising a receptive-responsive synergistic or co-creative relationship that dynamically involves both. This is the foundation for what has been called 'transfigural mathematics', which includes rather than excludes the inductive influence of receptive space as a dynamic inclusion of responsive information in natural energy flow.

Transfigural mathematics correspondingly considers the informational implications or *folds* of focal points of receptive space in natural energy flow. These focal points are known as zeroids (from *zero identities*), which are fundamentally unlike the dimensionless point masses and infinitesimals of conventional mathematics and physics, in that they are *breathing points*. Like tidal seas, they are capable of *volumetrically* taking in and emanating energy flows from and to the relative infinity of their immediate neighbourhood, which in turn is a dynamic inclusion of the oceanic neighbourhood of everywhere. They are points with characteristics of lines ('pointlines') and lines with characteristics of points ('linepoints') that ebb and flow as local informational spheres and channels of non-local spatial influence.

Spheres of Influence
What can it mean?
To Hold not to Have
In endearing relationship
Without vacant possession

A place to create
Content
Without being contained
In solitary confinement

Where walls have ears
That listen through echoes
Of resounding interludes
Passing beyond
Limited recall

Into the Zone
Of overlap
That continually beckons
From first to last
And last to first

Without completion
That corners the spirit
To cower or fight
In a boxing ring

Where the Bell tolls
For the End of the Round
Where we run aground
Awaiting Return

From beyond the strand line

Where fighting spirit
Is no longer required
To stand its ground
And protect itself
From heedless abuse

But floats like a butterfly
On current unseen
Without will or wish
To sting like a bee
Upon bended knee

Forced into submission
By inalienable Right
Angled to Poise
Above its own light
Cast down below

Where love creeps away
Vowing to return
But not fight
Another day

'Flow and Counterflow' (By Alan Rayner, Oil on canvas, 2008). *The continuous 'superchannel' of transfigural geometry spatially expands the discrete, one-dimensional, purely material line comprising*

contiguous but spatially discontinuous and dimensionless numerical point-masses upon which classical and modern mathematics are founded. Each discrete point is transfigured from a static, lifeless entity into a dynamic, breathing identity as a local informational (electromagnetic) sphere of non-local spatial influence, a 'breathing point'. The breathing points reciprocally inspire from and expire to their immediate neighbours, creating a double helical energy flow through coupled numerical neighbourhoods of three.

3. The Meaning of Natural Variety

Creative Intention
Here I account for the evolutionary origins and significance of natural variety and why a mechanism of selective favouritism cannot sustain or generate it.

Variety Observed at Gatwick
Evolution isn't intolerant of variety
Evolution cannot bear too many the same

Reproductive fitness is the antithesis of evolutionary fittingness
The opposite of what can be accommodated in sustainable flow

Swan Chemistry
We can't all be swans
Those ships of serenity
Whose surface appearance
Belies frantic pedalling
Beneath reflected view
To keep themselves on course

Where would swans be
In a world of their own
Without the babbles of ducks
Or twitters of warblers skulking in reeds?

Like a gathering of superstars
In supercilious congestion
Dead on their feet
Without the vulgarity
Needed to keep them flowing
By stirring the current

In common pools of correspondence
For all to breathe, including swans

Like noble gases
Semblances of calm
Amidst the swirling play of elements
Seeking satisfaction through the balancing of their orbits
Yet in that restless search for harmony
Needing to succeed only rarely
And never completely
If they are to keep the current stirred

Recreations of a Playful Universe
Oh, how we laugh!
When Some Thing
Touches Our Spirit
Tickles Our Imagination
Recalling Our Place
In a Playful Space

A common enjoyment
Of a Common Enjoinment
Recreations
Of an Ever Present
Folding

Dynamic Boundaries
Pivotal Places
Incomplete Surfaces
That make distinct
But Never Discrete

Unique and Special Identities
Possibilities Realized

That Can Never Be Bettered
And can never be Severed
From a Context Within and Beyond
That Makes Us Content
Belonging Together
Adoring Our Differences
Inseparable in Our Incompleteness

Our Self-Insufficiency
That Unites Us in Love
A Receptive Space
A No Thing Place
That Keeps Us Coherent
Within and Without
Enveloped and Enveloping

No Need For Rules
No Need For Rulers
With Space in Our Hearts
To Include Other as Us
A Diverse Assembly
A Joyous Relief
Reciprocating Each Other's Movements
Dancing in High Spirits

Oh, how we cry!
When Made To Deny
Our Union With Other
No Mother, No Brother
No Sister
To Assist
Our Passage
Through Pain

But a Father Severe
A Tyrant Authority
To Cut Us Off
Within Fixed Boundaries
In Isolation

Pretending Independence
Making Comparisons
Striving To Remove
What's Not Good Enough
In Pursuit of Perfection, Control, Prediction

A rationalistic Ideal
A Uniform Whole
A Self-Sufficiency
Tolerating No Hole
No Breathing Space
No Place for Grace

Demanding Reproduction
More of the Same
A Perpetual Cloning
With No Room to Err
No Room to Wander or Wonder

A Solid Object
With Space Outcast
An Infinite Outsider
Offering No Possibility
Of Excitement or Joy

A Purified Presence
A Divine Right
Freed From Wrong

An Unreal Abstraction
Motionless
Emotionless
Random Disunity
Divine DisContent

A Need For Rules
A Need For Rulers
No Space in Our Hearts
To Include Other as Us
A Monoculture
A Dull, Flat Field
Where Conflict Abounds

So, For Heaven's Sake, Father!
Take a Look at Your Wife!
Isn't She Sexy?
Get a Life!
Be Your Self!
Give Us Guidelines, By All Means
But, Please
Don't Hold Us Against Them

Stop Repeating Yourself!
Put Away Your Severing Knife!
Or, at the very least
Make a Hole that Heals
And Recreates –
Lets Us Play!

'Recreations' (Oil painting on canvas, by Alan Rayner, 2004).

Why Competition is a Big Myth Take

In *'The Screwtape Letters'*, from a senior devil to his apprentice, CS Lewis refers to 'the whole Philosophy of Hell' as resting

> ... *on a recognition of the axiom that one thing is not another thing, and, specifically, that one self is not another self. My good is my good and your good is yours. What one gains another loses. Even an inanimate object is what it is by excluding all other objects from the space it occupies; as it expands, it does so by pushing all other objects aside or by absorbing them. A self does the same. With beasts the absorption takes the form of eating; for us, it means the sucking of will and freedom out of a weaker self into a stronger. 'To be' means 'to be in competition'.*

By the sound of it, our modern human culture is utterly under the spell of this philosophy, along with its associated Darwinian and capitalist maxim that life is a struggle for existence in which we can only succeed by occupying a space or 'niche' in which we can prove ourselves fitter than and exploit others. This is a maxim that we teach ourselves to believe in throughout our education and business and governmental systems, scarcely stopping for a moment to reflect on whether it has a sound evidential or logical basis. If we did, we might come to realize that it is no more and no less than a convenient supposition, a simplistic figment of restrictive imagination that cannot do justice – indeed does great injustice – to the reality of natural evolutionary processes and our actual human experience of living and loving. But it has a very strong allure because it gives a sense of power over other, a false sense of freedom and security that can fortify self or group against the fearful uncertainty that lies beyond its immediate locality.

So, what could be wrong with the idea of being in competition? In a word: everything! To be in competition means to be in opposing, not complementary, relationship with the underlying objective being for one to gain or 'win' through the other's loss. This is the situation envisaged by Shakespeare's Hamlet, when he ponders:

To be or not to be, that is the question: whether 'tis nobler in the mind to suffer the slings and arrows of outrageous fortune, or to take arms against a sea of troubles, and by opposing end them?

The very idea of opposing things or forces depends *completely* on the assumed independence of matter from space such that the latter can come under the controlling influence of the former. Such independence ensures that any one thing or occupying agency is absolutely discontinuous from another thing in accordance with the definitive axiom known as 'the law of the excluded middle' upon which rests the *whole* philosophy of Hell.

But for such absolute discontinuity to hold, i.e. for there to be no continuity from one thing to another, the boundary between the inside and outside of each must be completely fixed and closed. That is, each thing must be a 'something' opposed to 'nothing', a completely definable 'object' or 'subject', which counts as an independent singularity or 'whole'. This is the paradoxical 'idealization' of natural form that is embedded in the numerical and geometrical foundations of classical and modern mathematics and objectivist science. The individual 'self' or 'set' must be an exception from its spatial neighbourhood in order to stand against, not be included within its 'sea of troubles'. Only by such means can someone or some group have the temerity to objectify himself or itself and other, and by so doing feel *free* to claim, as Albert Einstein did, that 'the environment is everything that isn't me', which opens the door to abuse of whatever is regarded as 'outside' as somewhere or something to lay waste.

Alas, poor Yorick: herein lies the whole source of the joy-killing nonsense upon which the myth of competition is constructed via the simplistic and arbitrary imposition of discrete limits upon natural energy flow! To be in opposition to other requires the presence of a discrete boundary. The presence of a discrete boundary prevents any communication or flow of energy across itself. So any discretely bounded entity is locked inside of itself and so inert with respect to its surroundings: its sole source of sustenance is internal. The closest that real live organisms get to such a condition is when they produce 'survival capsules' – spores, seeds, cysts, sclerotia, pupae etc – that enable them to suspend their animation under adverse circumstances. This is what real biological survival implies – not competing like Hell as energy availability diminishes, but entering a dormant phase that conserves what has already been assimilated. These dormant phases provide continuity within and between generations, which enables regeneration of growth potential through variably opening boundaries as energy availability increases.

There is no complete discontinuity in real organic life on Earth between genes, individuals, populations, communities and ecosystems; there is only continual reconfiguration of living system boundaries in a pool of space everywhere, through cycles of birth, growth, death and decay that correspond directly with the waxing and waning of energy supplies. It is the variable distribution of energy supply, not competition, which governs living patterns, processes and relationships. Organic life comes as a gift of predominantly solar energy via the infinite cosmos, which is packaged on Earth in finite but recyclable carbon. It is not a struggle for sovereign rights of ownership of local material resources. Matter cannot occupy space without closing itself down in frozen still life. Space permeates matter as it breathes in warmth and melts or dissolves into myriad distinguishable but not absolutely definable fluid dynamic forms of energy flow, some harder, some softer but none completely isolated within a permanent hard edge until or unless all possibility of opening closes.

So, what are the implications for a human culture that bases its thinking and governance on the paradoxical material independence from and control over space that underpins notions of competition and individual or group rights of ownership? In a few words, conflict, imperialism, eugenics, distress, loss of creativity, loss of loving relationship, selfishness, disintegration and unsustainable development out of phase with natural energy flows. Does this sound familiar? If so, what can we do about it – or, more to the point, what can we *stop* doing? I can only suggest that we stop competing with all and sundry, stop and think about the way we think, recognize the inadequacy of rationalistic logic and re-think about the truth of our natural situation, inconvenient as this might seem to be to manage or even speak about, let alone model mathematically.

The recently developed concepts of 'inclusionality', 'natural inclusion' and 'natural communion' offer a way out from the trap of objective rationality that leads to a competitive worldview, through recognizing that 'matter' and 'space' are mutually inclusive in natural energy flow, not mutually exclusive. Inclusionality can be described, but not defined, as a comprehension of nature as a fluid continuum of mutually inclusive informational (material) and spatial (immaterial) phases in which all form is flow-form, a dynamically receptive-responsive configuration of everywhere in somewhere, with no fixed centre. Natural inclusion is the co-creative, fluid dynamic transformation of all through all in receptive spatial context, whereby unique self-identity arises within the context of, not in isolation from, natural neighbourhood. Natural communion is the dynamic continuity of all nature in receptive spatial context, where all can be dynamically distinct and distinguishable, but none defined in absolute, independent singularity.

But, but, but, but, but, but, but, but..... I can hear the machine-gun fire of protestation resounding. Surely it's obvious that the natural world is full of competing organisms – just look at all those rutting stags, squabbling seagulls, spiky plants, confrontational robin redbreasts, antibiotic-producing fungi etc, etc. Anyway, look how far civilization has come technologically since the Stone Age and the surge of inventiveness during World War 2 – doesn't that *prove* objectivist science and social competition works!

But what *appears* to be an obvious interpretation of our observations can often arise from a *partial* (one-sided and prejudicial) way of seeing and underlying rationality, to which we human beings may be especially predisposed by our binocular vision, thumb-wielding facility for tool-use and huge inhibitory frontal brain lobes. For example, we (i.e. many of us) were content for centuries to interpret the *apparent* movement of the sun in terms of its circulation around a stationary Earth at the centre of the Universe. Moreover, we were able to construct an extraordinarily complicated mechanistic picture, the Ptolemaic system, based on this interpretation, and to use this without question or evident failure in our calendars, navigational aids and astronomic and astrological predictions. But eventually it just ceased to make good sense, i.e. to be consistent with evidence not supposition, and the less 'obvious' but simpler and more coherent Copernican system emerged. This did not need to include the *ad hoc* 'epicycles' used to explain the apparently erratic loop-the-loop paths of the planets or 'coincidence' to explain the 365 day periodicity in the cycles of movement of constellations. These now redundant explanations were quickly forgotten.

How, then, might an inclusional interpretation make more sense of natural evolutionary processes? To begin with, it can help by requiring neither an *ad hoc* stationary reference frame against and within which to plot the movements and spread of genes, organisms and populations, nor of definitive boundary limits within which paradoxically to isolate the variably permeable bodies of these local identities from their spatial neighbourhood. By the same token, it removes the need for either an external or an internal driving force, design or designer to bring about movement or evolutionary change, since these are implicit in the fluid logic and geometry of a natural energy flow in which matter and space are mutually inclusive. Correspondingly, it is fully consistent with evidence implicit in the development of contemporary scientific theories of relativity, quantum mechanics and non-linear dynamical systems, whilst removing the need for these latter to be framed mathematically within a fixed structure. It provides opportunity for new mathe-matical and scientific framings based on dynamic relational natural boundaries, not artificially imposed limits. It releases our creative potential from the distress of trying to live our lives as if these limits existed.

What, then, about all that 'obvious' aggression that we find in natural and human communities – how can this be understood if not in terms of competition? The point here is that apparent aggression need not signify *opposition* of one *against* other any more than the erosion of a river's bank need imply that the stream is at war with the landscape, or than the mountain ridge that forms at the watershed between two river basins implies that the two sides are at loggerheads. In natural flows there are confluences and divergences that can lead both to *differentiation* and *integration* of local identities depending on the quality and quantity of energy supply within and amongst the variably resistive and yielding interfacings of their spatial neigh-bourhood. Since these identities are *distinct but not discrete*, they neither strictly *compete* nor *co-operate*, but relate complementarily depending on their local situation, so as to balance their inflows and outflows in an energetically and evolutionarily sustainable way. Natural territorial boundaries are correspondingly the dynamic product of co-creative energetic interplay, which can help to protect and sustain local distinct identity and diversity, not an intention or requirement to join or eliminate opposing forces. The apparent consumption or replacement of one by another is not an act of forceful extermination of the former from somewhere to nowhere, but vital to natural processes of evolu-tionary reconfiguration and continuity that underlie all kinds of ecological succession and community development. Here death feeds life through the inclusion of space, life doesn't feed death through the exclusion of space upon which so much human conflict and waste is predicated.

Whereas differentiation and integration are therefore under-standable as natural processes contributing to the evolutionary diversity and complementary relationship of distinctive local informational identities in non-local space, competition and co-operation are – at least in the rationalistic sense these terms are usually used – artefacts of prescriptive definition. In this rational-istic sense, diversity itself becomes the enemy, a departure from 'ideal form' and 'line of best fit' that needs to be straightened out into conformity if life is to be made ordered, predictable and free from the conflict – not the rich complementary relationship – that comes of difference. Competition and conformity destroy the diversity and dynamic, synergistic relationship upon which evolution depends, in a hegemonic march to unsustainable monoculture whose influence on natural and human communities is cancerous.

In terms of the way we educate one another and embed this in the way we live and relate to one another and our surroundings, there is therefore a huge difference between competing with one another to achieve prescriptive targets defined by set standards or 'norms', and learning, through improvisation, to be receptive and responsive to diverse knowledge and viewpoints. The prescriptive, selective approach is restricted within its own rigid definitions as self-fulfilling prophecies, and so gets stuck with its apparent 'successes' whilst eliminating its 'failures' as worthless 'junk' into 'somewhere else'. Not only is it a source of profound distress and waste, but it is also unsustainable in the long run, where context is continually evolving. The improvisational, inclusional approach enables co-creative mutual understanding and transformation of all through all, in an evolutionarily sustainable way that respects and values diverse contributions to an ever-changing theme.

Hence there is nothing wrong with striving for excellence in dynamic relationship with others whose efforts can guide us – and who we can guide through our efforts – to appreciate the possibilities that reside within our uniquely situated and complementary personal identities. There is everything right in being able to differentiate and integrate between and amongst our diverse capabilities. But there is everything wrong in striving for supremacy within centres of complacency or 'ivory towers' that can look down with lofty arrogance and deep ignorance – at best with charity at worst with contempt – on the riff-raff of their natural neighbourhood.

So, now the 200th anniversary of Charles Darwin's birth has
passed by, perhaps we can celebrate both his wonderful recognition of the evolutionary kinship of all life, in all its diverse
natural communion, and deliverance from the diabolical,
hegemonic oxymoron of 'natural selection' as 'the preservation
of favoured races in the struggle for life'.

Breeding Intolerance
Wrinkles come
As wrinkles go
Immersed in the tolerance
Of the flow

That takes what comes
Within its stride
As natural rhythms
Of the tide

Covering and recovering
What lies both hidden
And exposed
In edges and ledges
Sandwiched between wedges
Of time in motion

Smoothing and fingering
Throughout each moment
Of tousled expression
That rises in falling
And falls in rising
Endlessly

Until some mind set on completion
Of its trip to Heaven's door

Instils the framework of conformity
To ease the comfort of its ride
By ruling out what comes and goes in wrinkles
In the breathing of the tide

And in that hard-line ruling
Constructs the basis of its case
For the defence of its indefensible
Discrimination between what it sees as fit
And what it doesn't
To preserve the interest of itself
As favourite subject
In the war that leads to wealth
At the cost of others' health

So begins selective breeding
To save the trouble of wearisome weeding
From the crop that grows against its grain
In ardent uniformity of production
That cannot dally in the valleys
Where wildness finds and forges shelter
And eases paths for others' play
But must impose its will to power
By insisting that it's Right
To be that way

But with that breeding comes intolerance
Of all that's needed when some day
The very ground on which the crop prevails
Can no longer bear the burden of its weight
And so begins to crack and crumple
Forming wrinkles coming and going
As the tide returns to flowing
And breathes a sigh of great relief

Harrowed Ground

The ground frowned
Its face shaved bare
From rich intertwinement
Of co-evolving variety
Nurtured Together
In receptive embrace

That bare-faced lying
Now cut with lines of worry
Its inner life disturbed and severed
To make way
For a new breed of aliens

Arrayed in rank file
Aspiring skywards
In vertical ascent
With no messing around
Underground or overground

But where now is that strange new breed?
Smothered by weed
That takes the space
Vacated by greed
A forlorn, foregone conclusion
Laid low by dis-ease
Born of its intrusive planting

Mocking Bird

Brick walls unite in solidarity
Or so I've heard
When their foundations
So absurd
Secured upon the very Word

That cuts their souls adrift
Feel the solvent waters
Lapping at their sound construction

I came across
One Such a Wall
Long and Straight
And Very Tall
Commanding the Waters
To Divide or Fall
And join the Ranks
Above It All

I tried to reason, softly
With the Wall
To allow some flecks a passage
Through its facade
So that it could flex
In resonant communion
Of One World With Its Other
A mutually corresponding Identity
Incompletely defined

But my words rebounded
In mocking echo
A harshly edited reflection
Of my dejection
A judgement of scorn
Not gladly borne beyond
Into dynamic Synthesis

I saw a bird
Bestride the Wall
Glorifying in the Sunder

Of It All

Looking first this way
Then That
Preening its coat of many colours
Calling Out in strident language

Don't you know
You stupid Fool
That Love's reception is not cool
When this is what It is
To be or not to be
Where It's At

The bird's forked tongue
Flickered freely
As it cast its spell
Of false dichotomy
Upon the nature of its source
In all around
I heard a rumbling
Far below
Some undercurrent
Of the Flow
In swirling eddies
Round the pillars
That Underpinned
The Wall's hard lining

So that it began
To Quake
And crumple
Stirred Up
By the shaky ground

Alarmed
The bird took flight
Into the open sky
Beyond the Wall

It wheeled and spiralled
Above my head
Dancing on some unseen softness
That brought it safely back to ground
To pick its way
And feed on life released
Amongst the rubble
That once had stood
In the way of One World and Its Mother

Until I caught a glimpse of being caught
In its glassy eye's reflection
And found
At last
A sign
Of welcome

All mocking gone

Path-finding and Path-Following: Spreading and Narrowing the Focus of Evolutionary Creativity through Natural Inclusion

Abstract

In planning for 'the future', much of our human focus continues to be on 'forward-thinking', which essentially relies upon projecting an historical record of the past into a trajectory that extends beyond the here and now. Trends are identified and short- and long-term objectives are set. These prescriptive 'targets' and 'best practices' are aimed for in an essentially linear progression along chains of cause and effect in a fixed, 3-dimensional framework that treats space and time as independent background constants. Biological evolution has been depicted in much the same way, as a process of progressive adaptation involving the preferential selection of those forms that have a competitive advantage in a defined set of circumstances or 'niche'.

Here I show how the rigid selectivity of this approach, whilst *simulating* one aspect of natural evolutionary processes, disregards another. It obstructs our ability to attune with an ever-changing context, such as that currently referred to as 'climate change'. For such attunement, a natural, evolutionarily-open process is necessary to enable a creatively receptive response in a space-including geometry that is fundamentally fluid, not fixed. This process of 'natural inclusion' involves the non-linear integration, differentiation and complementation of *both* radially symmetrical (all round) *and* polarized (channelled) non-local and local spatial information. Here, the latter is a dynamic inclusion – necessarily both including and included in the former, like a weathervane signifying airflow or fish attuning with a streambed. It cannot operate as an independent executive object, isolated from what includes itself.

Fixing the Future: Goal-Oriented Rationality in a Euclidean Frame
Imagine you are one of a party of survivors of a plane crash in the middle of a desert. Somewhere, beyond your immediate view, there *may* be an oasis. How might you find refreshment? In this essay, I show why, in such a situation, a single-minded, Darwinian, 'survival of the fittest' mentality would be disastrous, and how a fungus, or any similar fluid dynamic natural organization could do better with no evident selective consciousness or central executive leadership. I go on to explore how, notwithstanding our self-awareness, our human ability to love our neighbourhood as our 'self' may make us more creatively like a fungus

than we might *think* we are!

A singular characteristic of human perception appears to be the widespread idea that somehow some 'thing' objectively called 'the future' exists, which can be approached along a predetermined path that leads predictably to either a 'good' or a 'bad' end. Those elite few empowered through this perception to be 'decision-makers' on behalf of the populace hence stake their claims to authority upon their ability to select which path will have a good outcome and ensure that it is followed by means of suitable legislation and enforcement. What counts as 'good' depends, however, on making a 'value-judgement', a matter of opinion concerning relative desirability that may or may not be shared by all concerned. Even where some kind of electorate is consulted, the outcome may not be 'democratic' in the sense of governance for all by all, but rather the imposition of rule by a majority, whose favour is curried by rhetorical debate. A sharp dividing line develops between 'them' and 'us', those empowered or oppressed by the system. Conflict and tension become inevitable, especially where what are judged by those with power to be desirable ends are used to justify undesirable means applied to those oppressed.

The pursuit of desirable objectives itself depends upon a system of objective logic, perhaps unique to human beings, whereby 'good' or 'bad' are defined in absolute moral terms, regardless of natural situation. Indeed this logic has the effect of placing a hard dividing line between 'human being' and 'other nature'. The latter then becomes what externally threatens or serves human interest, not what human interest inextricably both includes and is included by as natural neighbourhood. For at the heart of this logic is the strict definition of 'what is' *or* 'is not' a particular object. Any 'middle ground' between what *is* and *is not* is thereby explicitly excluded – the so-called 'law of the excluded middle'. Ultimately, this law depends on the exclusion of 'space' – as constant empty background or 'void' – from 'matter' – as condensed electromagnetic information or 'energy'.

The exclusion of immaterial from material presence – rather than dynamic mutual inclusion of each in and by the other – leads to a de-spirited, static, purely materialistic view of natural form shaped by 'structure' alone. Here, 'space', is paradoxically regarded both as 'absence of quantifiable material presence' and as 'distance' between material entities, which is measured in terms of structural units of length, area and volume. In other words space is measured in units of structure, whilst counting as nothing in itself, a nonentity and non-participant in the dynamics of independent form, contained in a box of x, y and z co-ordinates extending from zero through infinitesimal to infinite. Within this box, movement can only be brought about through the imposition of 'force', ultimately derived from somewhere ineffable, rather than being implicitly included in a continual natural process of contextual transformation (see Rayner 2004).

This is the cubical cubicle world of 3-dimensional Euclidean geometry, where points are dimensionless, lines are width-less, planes are depthless and solids are pure magic! The great arith-metical convenience of this world is that both space and time can be abstracted as constants, divisible into discrete equal units to form an independent reference frame in which to fix and quantify the movements, mass and numbers of pure material objects. Curvature is not treated as natural or primary, but constructed secondarily by calculus, in infinitesimal steps from discrete point masses or singularities. Acceleration is derived from velocity, not vice versa.

Only in this back-projected, atomized world of alienation of material from immaterial presence can any kind of fixed independent form exist, for any natural curvature implies a dynamic spatial asymmetry (inequality) between interdependent concave and convex domains. These domains are reciprocally coupled and distinguished through the transition zone or 'boundary' that simultaneously outlines one and inlines the other. Try to blow a cubical bubble and you'll gather what I mean!

As was recognized by Henri Poincaré (1905), it takes only a few moments' real-world consideration to appreciate that this *primarily* linear world of Euclidean geometry is inconsistent with our living experience of nature as inhabitants of the varied dynamic surface of a space-including sphere with no fixed centre or corners. It is both an abstraction from and an inverted supranatural imposition upon real-world dynamic geometry. Yet it lies deep in the heart of the fallacious and ultimately adversarial, distressing and addictive logic that we[2] apply so rigorously to our understanding of life on Earth. What is it about human beings, which makes us so susceptible to becoming entrapped by this pure materialistic logic?

Abstract Sovereignty: The Unnatural Selectivity of Hierarchical Governance

Imagine for a moment that you are not a member of a party, but a sole survivor of that plane crash in the desert. Your only hope, quite literally, is to set as straight a course as you can for the horizon. You proceed with grim determination, looking forward all the way, as we humans are predisposed to do through eyes set on the front of our faces and powerful frontal lobes in our brains, which repress any sideways distraction of conscious attention from our fixed objective. You are further aided by your own footprints, which help you to avoid departing from or backtracking along your initially-set trajectory, and any set reference points like a distant hilltop or the trajectory and angle of elevation of the sun. At last, water appears in the distance. You thank God and/or congratulate your own single-mindedness for your deliverance. Of course, for all you know, you *could* have set off in exactly the wrong direction, but then you wouldn't have lived to tell the tale. So you prepare to repeat this successful strategy, thinking that what's served you so well in 'the past' will serve you equally well in 'the future'.

It's easy in this context to understand how the human tendency to fixate upon desirable objectives can be developed and reinforced by any sense of individual isolation in a desolate, unyielding landscape. Here, the only immediate sign of 'life' or 'movement' is within one self and all else appears to be fixed structure and empty space. The doublethink begins to emerge of the individual as a 'free agency' – a local, self-centred automaton paradoxically driven *either* by internal purpose *or* external force and free to do whatever it thinks fit in order to stay alive and well. This is the thought that appears to have become deeply entrenched in modern human culture, reinforced along its way by philosophical, religious, mathematical, scientific, educational, political and economic orthodoxy ('right-mindedness'). Moreover, there is strong anthropological evidence that this thought began its ascent to prominence with 'The Fall', during a period around 6000 years ago, when large areas of the Middle East and North Africa became desert (Taylor, 2005).

Our dislocated sense of self-centredness as ghost-in-the-machine prisoners of our skin, severed from and hence in rivalry with the world of other(s) outside, has us seek to impose our will upon this world in a superhuman effort to avoid being overwhelmed by it. We struggle for our existence through seeking sovereignty over other(s).

We begin to divide the world and ourselves up into opposing factions and fractions, which can only be overruled by the power of 'higher authority'. We seek the rich rewards this power brings for ourselves. We gain this power by winning competitive games of one against another. But as we do so, the possibility of loving 'other' as a vital aspect of our 'self' recedes further and further and further away, behind the barricade that we have ourselves set against it.

Our creative lives become diminished, fearful and ultimately as desolate as the desert mindset that drove us to such abstraction. The most help we can expect from others in our human neighbourhood is to co-preserve an uneasy balance of power. We survive but don't thrive, armed to the teeth with weapons of mutually assured destruction and certain of our mutual selfishness and mistrust worthiness, in accordance with John Nash's 'Game Theory' and Richard Dawkins' 'Selfish Genes'. Many of us may try to escape this unforgiving world through various forms of addiction and expressions of mental distress. Meanwhile, we let our living space go to pot, until, as recently, we suddenly notice that it's overheating, and frantically set about trying to rectify it using the same sovereign logic that got us into trouble in the first place. Over thirty years ago, when I was depressed following a year of postgraduate research in which I had been fully exposed for the first time in my life to the real implications of 'objective scientific method', I portrayed this desolation in the painting shown below.

'**Arid Confrontation**' (Oil painting on board, by Alan Rayner, 1973). *This painting depicts the limitations of the detached view of the observer excommunicated from nature. After a long pilgrimage, access*

to life is barred from the objective stare by the rigidity of artificial boundaries. A sun composed of semicircle and triangles is caught between straight lines and weeps sun-drops into a canalized watercourse. Moonlight, transformed into penetrating shafts of fear, encroaches across the night sky above a plain of desolation. Life is withdrawn behind closed doors.

No Fixed Limits: Fluid Dynamic Patterns of Natural Exploration
How very different it could all be if instead of being a sole survivor in the desert, we were members of a party who could radiate in all directions, whilst remaining in touch with one another visually, acoustically and/or via our paths in the sand. When any one or a few of us came within range of an oasis, we could immediately communicate this to our nearest neighbours. Our neighbours would relay the message to their neighbours, and all would quickly converge upon and reinforce our initial path, some crossing over from, others retracing their original footsteps. We'd all arrive at the oasis more or less together and splash ourselves all over in delight. We might chatter excitedly and praise our human cleverness for devising such a successful survival strategy. But then we'd be wrong. For such spreading and narrowing of focus in dynamic attunement with spatial context is characteristic of all kinds of living flow-forms, including fungi, as shown below. In fact it's characteristic of flow-forms generally, not just those we have become accustomed to classify as 'life as we know it' on Earth.

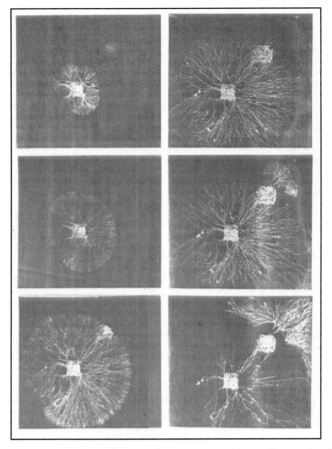

'Fungal Foraging'. *A fungus finds an oasis in a desert, by fluid-dynamically spreading and narrowing its energetic focus. The wood-decaying fungus,* Hypholoma fasciculare, *has been inoculated into a tray full of soil on a block of wood ('starter' food source), with an uncolonized wood block ('bait' food source) placed some distance away from it. Distinct stages are shown in the radial spreading of the fungal colony from the inoculated wood block, followed by the redistribution and focusing of its energy in one direction following upon contact with the bait. Similar fluid dynamic patterns of gathering in, conservation of, exploration for and redistribution of energy supplies are found throughout the living world, from subcellular to ecosystem scales of organization (From Dowson et al., 1986; see also Rayner, 1997).*

Now just imagine that when the first of the party of plane crash survivors to locate an oasis refused to communicate with his or her neighbours but instead rushed headlong to take sole advantage. Alternatively, imagine that the leader of the advance party claimed ownership over the find, saying that it was down to their superiority over their neighbours, and formed a posse to defend and perhaps charge an entrance fee to the facility. What kind of betrayal would that be? How much betrayal of that kind is evident in modern human culture and survival of the fittest mentality?

The relationship between spread-focus and narrow-focus exploration is also evident in two distinctive patterns of human brain activity, closely associated with creativity. These are called the Inspiration and Elaboration phase (e.g. see Claxton, 2006).

In the Inspiration phase, there is openness to all kinds of possibility via an unconditional panoramic perceptive process associated with 'alpha waves' in the brain. For many people this process may be taken for granted or unconscious – indeed associated with dreaming or daydreaming. Personally, however, I am very aware of consciously allowing myself to become receptive to whatever comes, by relaxing both my body and frame of mind as I give free rein to my imagination prior to setting to work on a piece of writing or painting or problem or opportunity. As inspiration is gained, particular possibilities are developed and refined into explicit form through the Elaboration phase, a process characterized by 'beta waves' associated with strong activity of the frontal lobes of the brain, which concentrate attention along a particular avenue.

These phases may also be related to distinctive forms of sensory perception, musculature and emotions. The Elaboration phase of unidirectional thought would correspond with attraction or repulsion responses to or from sources of fear and satiation, detected through our explicit senses of sight, sound, taste, smell and touch, and mediated through 'tonic' or 'fast action' muscle fibres. The Inspiration phase of omni-directional thought would correspond with feelings of comfort and discomfort, derived from implicit all-round bodily 'proprioception' or 'situational awareness' of gravitational and thermal fields, and mediated through 'phasic' or 'slow action' muscle fibres. Whereas Inspiration provides an awareness of inclusion in 'everywhere' (non-local), Elaboration directs attention to 'somewhere' (local).

Clearly, these phases of inspiration and elaboration are complementary and interdependent, not mutually incompatible. Neither alone can amount to much: inspiration without elaboration is incoherent; elaboration without inspiration is restrictive. Moreover, the linear – directional – view can be derived from the non-linear – panoramic – by closing down spatial possibility, but not vice versa. The linear has to open up to the inclusion of space everywhere – all in all – to melt into non-linear.

What a travesty it is, then, if the linear view becomes regarded as somehow superior to and given inverted precedence over the non-linear! Yet just such favouritism is evident in an immense variety of hierarchically structured human walks of life, as well as in our selective interpretation of history and evolutionary process through post-hoc 'hindsight'. A linear path is back-projected from present into past, and only those events or characters that occur sequentially along this path are acknowledged to have contributed to the historical lineage of cause and effect. The path becomes a regression 'line of best fit', selected through the exclusion of other possibilities, which become regarded as 'peripheral', 'vulgar', 'non-mainstream' or even as wasteful 'failures'. Correspondingly, conventional neo-Darwinian evolutionary theory describes a process of 'preserving the best and discarding the rest' of a randomly generated set of variations, as if 'success' were a prescriptively fixed target that could only be attained in one way.

From such thinking emerges the idea that 'if only I/we could predict with foresight the path to success that is evident from hindsight, how much better off I/we would be'. This is the idea that leads us to impose prescriptive closure upon our objectives and hence narrow down our creative options when trying to plan ahead, ever fearful of succumbing to competition with our rivals as the penalty for 'error' or 'failure'. We become path-followers, not pathfinders: tunnel vision begets tunnel vision in an ever-deepening rut.

Close inspection of 'fungal foraging' reveals, however, that this selective understanding of evolutionary process literally presents a very partial, elitist and wasteful view of what really happens, even where there is a fixed 'target', let alone when opportunity is continually shifting via the transformation of the contextual landscape. Far from being excluded as 'failures' from the path of discovery, the energetic resources initially spread out along other paths are gathered back into it, enabling considerable amplification. Simplification is achieved not by eliminative selection, but by integrative inclusion, involving the co-creative, fluid dynamic transformation of all by all in the receptive spatial context of labyrinthine pathways that become less resistive to current as current flows along them, enabling autocatalytic flow. Herein lies the fundamental difference between evolution by (un)natural selection – as an essentially degenerative process of ever-diminishing competitive options in a restrictive domain – and evolution by natural inclusion, as a creative process of ever-opening possibilities in a transforming spatial context.

Whirls, Curls, Nests and Labyrinths: The Dynamic, Space-including Geometry of Natural Inclusion

Geometrically, then, what makes the difference between a generative and degenerative evolutionary process is the dynamic inclusion, in the former, of space as 'omnipresence of structural absence'. This inclusion is vital in the formation of a variable viscosity, variable permeability field of dynamic relational curvature in which every concavity simultaneously and reciprocally implies a convexity over nested scales from subatomic to universal. In this field any displacement of 'somewhere' local *simultaneously* and *reciprocally* implies a transformation in the configuration (i.e. a 'transfiguration') of 'everywhere' non-local, and vice versa. 'Content' cannot change or move independently of the spatial context of which it is a dynamic inclusion. Evolution involves the continual harmonizing ('dynamic balancing', 'attunement' or 'resonance') of local with non-local, not the perfection of individual fixed entities through one-way 'adaptation' to a fixed 'other'.

The mutual correspondence of ever transforming convex and concave via necessarily incomplete and hence 'holey' or permeable, intermediary domains implies a fundamental dynamic geometry of Nature. This geometry extends from microcosm to macrocosm and differs radically from the hard-line abstractions of Euclid. It is *primarily* non-linear or curved, due to the inductive receptivity of spatial attraction, giving rise to spheres, ellipsoids, spirals and tubes.

Linear structure emerges *secondarily* from this geometry, as in the cylinders formed by trees or the hexagonal arrays formed in honeycombs and the regular surfaces of crystals. This natural geometry is also 'nested', with smaller domains contained within and communicating with larger domains. The simplest form of expression of this geometry would be a set of concentric perforated spheres, but has the potential to become extremely 'involved' or 'complex'.

The nearest approach that conventionally fixed-framed mathematics has made to this natural fluid dynamic geometry of 'nested holeyness' or 'holey communion' is known as 'fractal geometry'. This was made famous by Benoit Mandelbrot (1977) as a way to describe structures whose boundaries, unlike Euclidean surfaces, appear progressively more complex/

irregular, in 'self-similar' patterns, the closer they are observed. Almost anything we look at in nature from clouds, to snowflakes, to river valleys, to ferns, to trees, to lungs has this property, which makes them immeasurable in terms of discrete units of length, area and volume, because how much you see depends on how close you are. For example, the length of the coastline of Madagascar seems much less to an astronaut orbiting the Earth than it does to a mite crawling around its many indentations. At infinitesimal scales of closeness, the length is infinite.

The problem of quantifying fractal structures can be solved by relinquishing the Euclidean idealization that dimensions can have only integral values of 0, 1, 2, 3, 4 etc, and allowing them also to have fractional (hence 'fractal') values. The fractal dimension of a structure can be calculated from the equation:

$$M = kr^D$$

where M is the material 'content' of a portion of the structure, r is the radius of the field in which this portion of content is contained, and D is the dimension. D can readily be found from the relationship between the logarithms of M and r for different fields of view. If the structure is homogeneous, then D will have an integral value. If it is heterogeneous, D will be fractional.

Fractal patterns can be simulated mathematically by iterating non-linear equations. A famous example is the 'Mandelbrot set' itself, which appeared in many guises as a colourful modern mathematical art form in the late twentieth century. This set is made by mapping the distribution of points in the 'complex plane' that do not result in infinity when iterated according to the rule, $z \rightarrow z^2 + c$, where z begins at zero and c is the complex number corresponding to the point being tested. Here, a 'complex number' is a number that consists of a combination of a 'real' and 'imaginary' component, the latter being a derivation of 'i', the square root of -1. The complex plane is formed in the space defined by placing all 'real' numbers, from -∞, through 0, to +∞ along a horizontal line, and all 'imaginary' numbers, from -∞i, through 0, to +∞i, along a vertical line, and using these Euclidean lines as co-ordinates. In effect, it represents a way of increasing the 'possibility space' for numbers as discrete entities to inhabit, from one to two dimensions.

The remarkable feature of the Mandelbrot set is the extraordinarily complex boundary that occurs between points within and points outside the set, in effect between an inner attractive space of zero and an outer attractive space of infinity. Such complex boundaries formed between neighbouring attractive spaces or 'attractors' have more generally been referred to as 'fractal basin boundaries', and are clearly at least analogous to the complex boundaries of natural process geometry. The conventional abstract mathematical representation of such complexity, however, *begins* prescriptively with the implicit or explicit Euclidean or numerical *definition* of contents and containers as complete *wholes*, hence retaining paradoxical singularity and replacing their *simultaneous* reciprocal relationship with *sequential* 'feedback'. Natural geometry, by contrast, implies intermediary, incompletely definable realms (dynamic boundaries) through which convex and concave spatial possibilities are coupled and transformed by one another. Endless creative possibility emerges.

Simplifying Agenda: Removing the Complication from Complexity Theory

The *complex involvement* of 'all in the fluid dynamic field of all' may appear quite off-putting to those of us who yearn for a 'simple life', as well as impossible to analyse or study comprehensively by those striving for the clarity of rationalistic objectivity. Yet at the heart of this involvement is an underlying simplicity of dynamic local/non-local relationship, which has not been accounted for explicitly in modern Complexity Theory based on the 'self-organization' of many-bodied systems (e.g. Goodwin, 1994). This simplicity is actually obscured by efforts to simplify Nature via the imposition of a fixed reference frame or boundary limit around discrete objects or groups of objects. For in a real-world geometry where no such frame or discrete boundary is known to exist, to impose it can only ultimately add in redundant complication, distortion and misunderstanding. In much the same way, the complicated 'epicycles' used to explain 'erratic' planetary movements in the Ptolemaic, geocentric model of the solar system made life Hell for students and scholars of astronomy prior to the Copernican Revolution. Perhaps it is opportune now to remove this frame, or at least use it wisely, purely as a tool of enquiry rather than as an end in itself. Maybe we should focus instead on real-world dynamic boundaries as our source of reference to where we are in the scheme of every-where, integral as these boundaries are in the fluid pooling together of all in all, microcosm in macrocosm and vice versa.

Dynamic Balancing: The Non-Executive Management of Natural Neighbourhood

There is a form of leadership that does not call for a careful, creative and reflective consideration of possibilities viewed from all angles by all concerned. Rather, it demands conformity with its own vision and specification of destination. In the absence of others' agreement, it carries on regardless with whatever *action* it has planned, convinced in its own mindset that this is the 'right *thing* to do'. Any leader of this ilk, whether elected by a supposedly democratic majority or not, considers him or herself to have a prerogative to do what they *know* to be best for the world, regardless of context. Moreover, by exercising their moral imperialism in the face of opposition they demonstrate the strength of their authority, a resolve that historical narrative will, they imagine, in due course affirm and celebrate. But events often don't exactly turn out as predicted. The real life and death situation on the ground is far more complex and non-linear than envisaged. The effects of intervention in complex – highly involved – situations aren't so certain in the long run. The ensuing tragedies are never more heart-rending than when a leader decides to declare war upon his neighbourhood.

This is a style that I think is all too commonly the *sole* form of leadership recognized in human organizations: a product of prescriptively definitive (rationalistic) thinking and action that places deterministic power at control centres or hubs. It amounts to what might be called *authoritarian, dictatorial, proprietorial* or, as my correspondent Ted Lumley puts it, *powerboat* leadership. It entails leadership towards a set destination of a fleet of individuals that have declared themselves independent of their natural situation by dint of strapping an outboard motor of technology on their backsides. It creates one Hell of a wash of collateral damage for those caught up in its turbulence. It is the kind of leadership provided by *some* so-called experts, gurus, presidents and ministers whose actions primarily serve individual self-interest, whereby an individual or elite lays down the law or 'codes of conduct' for others to follow, regardless of circumstances.

There is, however, another style of leadership, or perhaps more aptly, *craftsmanship*, that seeks to cultivate creative space for all to air their views and benefit from shared experience. This is what might be called *Arthurian* (after King Arthur and the Knights of the Round Table), *co-educational, non-proprietorial* or, as Ted Lumley puts it, *sailboat* leadership. Such craftsmanship is based on learning through experience how to attune with natural processes, in a way that all can learn from.

Now, as the supposedly 'United Nations' of humanity contemplates its 'next steps', in the face of seemingly global environmental, psychological and social crisis, the question of which, if either, of these forms of leadership is wiser seems very important. Here, it is not a question necessarily of 'which is better?' in an 'either/or' sense, but how can these styles best be balanced? How does anyone in this situation who seeks leadership or has leadership thrust upon them, see their role? Do they see themselves as co-cultivators of creative space for wise enquiry? Do they see themselves as Directors and Proprietors of organizations? Is wise leadership something definable that we can be *instructed* about via the 'right kind of training' in a real or virtual Institution? Is wise leadership perhaps identifiable with *love*, some indefinable presence that we can open ourselves to and co-cultivate?

Beneath all, I am suggesting that we need to learn or re-learn how to live and love a little more, and conflict a lot less, if we are to attune co-creatively with our ever-transforming natural neighbourhood. But I can no more tell you prescriptively how to 'do' this than I can tell you how to ride a bicycle along a bumpy road. I can only show and encourage you in a non-executive way that it's possible, by relaxing your self-definition and *using your feeling*. In much the same way, with no need for an onboard computer or set of gradient-detecting instruments, a weathervane aligns through its *bodily* relationship with airflow, and a trout orients with streambed. It's easy if you don't try too hard.

Sectored Communion -

Three poems inspired by Jack Whitehead's description of a disturbing experience in Bali:

> *Seeing the road sign in Bali and then standing in the large courtyard with the five paths leading to a Mosque, Hindu Temple, Buddhist Temple, Catholic Church and Anglican Church brought thoughts to mind of inclusional humanity and the problem of different faiths finding their unity in worship/submission to different Gods in ways that excluded those who did not profess their form of worship/submission.*
>
> *The bombing on Jimbaran Beach of the spot where Joan and I had*

eaten three weeks earlier brought into stark relief some of the
damaging/lethal responses of fundamentalist intransigence
– Jack Whitehead

'Road Sign in Bali' (photograph by Jack Whitehead).

What struck me about this experience, and the way Jack described it, was the irony that each faith might lock 'outside in the courtyard' what they each worshiped in common but in their culturally distinctive ways. By so doing they could harden the fluid lines of mutual distinction and complementary relationship that are characteristic of naturally diverse communities into abstract 'hard lines of definition' that impose unnatural conformity and alienation of 'others'. The devastating implications of such needless alienation – which is to be found both within and between secular and theistic human communities – were evident in the scene on the beach. Yet in recognising the roots – ultimately to be found in the *assumption that space stops and starts at discrete boundary limits* – of the intransigence from which that atrocity erupted, lies also the hope for the future of human communities in which both natural variety and what holds this variety in common are valued.

The Divisive Loyalties of Estranged Alliances – and Their Urgent Need for Solvation

From the Infinite Openness
Where each lived In the Love of the Other
Like foetus in Mother
Caressed by the Natural Communion
Of soul in Spirit
And spirit in Soul
Dynamically encapsulated
In fluid bodily linings

Led Five Discrete Paths
Each to a building block
Of Its own making
With doors closed
To any who'd cross between one and the other
Through the openness
That pooled all in all

Down the drains
Of those estranged alliances
Many poured
Bonded together
By what held them inside
Or, woe betide

Each seeking portals
To the path of righteousness
Down which they'd travelled
To lock outside

But in that quest
Believing it best
To Blast the Hell

Out of One Another
Instead of dissolving the walls
That held them as thralls.

Blocked by Intransigence
The river paused and brooded
Along her windy, winding course
Blockaded yet again
By thick intransigence
Sharpened into concrete dams
Set in opposition to her flow
By minds determined to preserve their status
As statues standing for the status quo
In a State where love and life are enemies
The ever-present fearful foe
Of corrupting force

Where now?
The river pondered
In the dull stagnation of house arrest
Where spirit crumbles as soul festers
Enforced to kerb her ardour
In underground dwelling
Far from the fields
She longed to burst with lovely life

Still, she laid the tables
Ready for whoever
Might find their way
Past the dust and crust
Of arid confrontation
To feast on her delightful preparation
For thirsty, hungry travellers
To chance upon her hidden presence

Only to find that those she nurtured
Once they had taken their greedy fill
Burst back into the glare of publicity
Beaming with the satisfaction of their discovery
To claim it for themselves

Denying where they had found her
Shutting her up with loud-mouthed declarations
Protesting their right to vacant possession of her heart
Until, at last, her pulse fluttered and faded

Leaving them stranded on those summits
From which they'd crowed
Striving to escape the heat of their dereliction
By ascending to the Heavens

Never imagining for a moment
That all they had to do
To bring her back to life
Was dig down deeper
Through the crusts they'd layered
Over her poor, stilled body
To release the Springs from which she'd journey
Creating valleys for her current
Celebrated now in broad daylight.

A Cruel Sort of Faith
What sort of faith is it
That shuts Him outside
By refusing to welcome
Her into our midst?

Only a cruel sort of faith
That sorts us into categories

Transforming the Love of our Life
Into the hatred of objects for subjects
Alienated by definition

Where none can flow
Through each in the other
But sticks instead
To its own side of the bed
With body guillotined
From head

Allowing blithe Spirit
To wander free
Unconcerned
For what calls out
From bended knee
To release the pain of anxiety

That fearful dread
Of what's beneath the bed
Lurking in Shadow
Beyond light's reach
The Lost Soul Longing
For re-admission

'Willowy Bridge' (Oil painting on board by Alan Rayner, 1974). *The chasm between the left and right worlds of hawkish and serene natures is conjoined by what brings each into the mutual influence of the other, allowing soulful passage through the veil in their midst.*

Evolution without Paradox – The Improvisational Continuity of Natural Inclusion

Any attempt to explain or model a continuous process on the basis of discontinuous logic and mathematics cannot fail to be paradoxical. This is because as soon as any event, entity or objective is rationalistically singled out from the fluid continuum by placing it within a definitive frame of reference, the process itself stalls. It is akin to localizing a changing scene within the fixed frames of a cine film and then using the frames as the basis for explaining or predicting *the very movement that they arrest* into discrete segments of space and time. The *apparent* continuity that meets the eye in the projected string of images is no more than the product of *contiguity* or 'informational adjacency', not the true *continuity* of what goes missing beyond the edges and in the gaps between each frame. Correspondingly, the *apparent* movement in the projected sequence is nothing less than a string of imaginative leaps of faith across chasms of space confined between the trammels of a linear path or trajectory.

Nonetheless, such backwards or forwards linear projections continue to be accepted not just as a valuable tool of investigative enquiry, but as a legitimate way of accounting *completely* for the past and predicting the future based on exact local knowledge of the present. In effect, the 'progress' of discrete 'objects' pushed or pulled by external or internal forces is plotted from 'here' to 'there' along a 'timeline' divided up into equal and sequential intervals. The outcome is not only a very inadequate, misleading and logically inconsistent Newtonian/neo-Darwinian explication of the evolution of life, but a psychologically, socially and environmentally damaging perception of our human place on Earth. This is the source of needless senselessness, distress, conflict, inefficiency and loss of creativity that it really would be good for us to assign to history. In the process, we could open up and sustain the possibility for a more varied, tolerant, just, compassionate, democratic and enjoyable future for ourselves and their natural human neighbourhood.

The assumption that the 'present' is the product of its immediately preceding 'time frame', and that the future is completely prescribed by the present lies deep in the discontinuous logical and mathematical foundations of *deterministic* evolutionary models. These are *'evolution in a box'* models, which start by defining 'the initial conditions' or 'niche' that change is going to be constrained within, by dint of internal genetic information content ('nature') and/or external environmental imposition ('nurture'), and proceed to account for how these conditions are fulfilled. Whatever happens is pre-ordained as the box becomes filled by whatever fits it best, if needs be through the competitive exclusion of others. There is no room for manoeuvre here, no role for individual creativity or 'choice' in what happens and ultimately, therefore, no responsibility to be accepted or claimed other than that of the box 'designer', whether natural or supernatural, intelligent or stupid. Those that fit the box are accepted as 'successes', those that don't are discarded as 'failures'. Once in occupation, the occupant stays as it is, running at a standstill like the proverbial 'Red Queen', because to change would be 'non-adaptive' in the short term, unless the 'designer' so happens to pop another box magically alongside the one already occupied. Far from providing the foundation for expression of natural variety and evolutionary creativity, these models paradoxically remove and stall them into 'fixation'. They then rely on 'random accidents' inconsistent with their prescriptive limits to engender the possibility of a staccato pattern of change that lurches discontinuously and wastefully from pillar to post. An incredible, digital 'to be or not to be' story of 'missing links' and 'impossible odds' unfolds between atomic simplicity and biological complexity, delivered down to the faithful from the ivory-towered authority of their leaders.

The application of these prescriptive evolutionary models to human 'forward planning' is all too evident in those many kinds of 'agenda' that fix a desirable 'objective' or 'end' in advance, regardless of changeable circumstances, and proceed to fulfil this at all costs and by whatever 'means' deemed necessary. Everything and everyone is selected to fit its purpose according to the agenda, on pain of being discarded as 'not good enough'. Schoolchildren are uniformed and examined relentlessly for their ability to reproduce what they are told. Jobseekers are required to fit job descriptions, not the other way round. Members of Parliament, those supposedly democratic representatives of the people, are punished if they don't conform to their Party Whip. Research Projects are required to predict their findings in order to receive funding, and regarded as failures if they discover something different, no matter how innovative. Heretics, who honestly stand up for what they think is true, are ostracized or worse. And so the paradoxical logic of discontinuity perpetuates itself, neither grounded in evidence nor sound sense, but rooted instead in a convenient supposition that serves the self-interest of the powerful and is easy to fabricate into stories acceptable, especially given the carrot and stick of reward and punishment, to the gullible. We set ourselves on course for an evolutionary dead end governed by the rule of selfish ascendance.

No sooner, however, is the rationalistic logic of discontinuity recognized for what it is, as the mythical product of assuming that material form can be singled out from the context of open space that it both dynamically includes and is included in, than a very different way of understanding evolutionary process emerges. Evolution breaks free from the box of predestination and opens out into the continual, improvisational process of 'natural inclusion' as the co-creative, fluid dynamic transformation of all, through all, in receptive spatial context'.

This process is based on the continuous logic of inclusionality, which lies in the understanding of natural energy flow as the dynamic inclusion of space in form and form in space. 'Space' is understood here not as a rationalistic 'emptiness' or 'absence of presence' that counts as 'nothing', but instead as limitless 'openness'. Far from being a source of 'discontinuity', which stops at the surface of perceptible form, space is that infinite, uncontainable, indivisible and hence continuous omnipresence that pervades throughout everywhere and pools all together. As a dynamic inclusion of form, space has a receptive quality, and as a dynamic configuration of space, form has responsive, protective and reflective qualities. Instead of being regarded, like a cine film frame, as a purely local and definable space-excluding or containing object that can at most be connected contiguously to others, all form is understood as 'flow-form', a dynamic locality or 'somewhere' as an inclusion of 'everywhere', non-local. Every flow-form is correspondingly a receptive-reflective-responsive opening or 'hole' that is included in the flow of every other form, like eddies in a river. It cannot be a 'whole' or even a part of a 'whole', complete in itself, and only rigidifies into stasis when frozen in or crystallized – whereupon its fluid mobility can only be restored by melting or dissolving.

Hence the evolutionary process is more like a river for all to immerse in and contribute to, than an arrow of time for the select favoured few to progress along. There is neither complete end nor complete beginning to the river, for in its dynamic inclusion of infinite openness it continues to open up and follow new possibilities for flow within its ever-changing catchment. As individual dynamic bodily localities we can accept our lives as a gift of natural energy flow from others and relay this on to others when necessary in a continual co-creative circulation instead of a competitive dash of opponents to the finishing line. Where and how and in what form the river will travel is unpredictable in the long run, for uncertainty is inevitable where the inclusion of infinite possibility precludes the complete definition of initial conditions and all are simultaneously included in each others' influence. But that uncertainty doesn't preclude understanding of the possibilities and attunement to changing circumstances in an evolutionarily and environmentally sustainable way. It is only when we step out of the river, claiming immunity from its and one another's influence, that we set ourselves on course for a dead end, wasting talent and energy in a relentless quest for the false security and meaningless freedom of uniformity.

In coming to recognize our dynamic inclusion in natural evolutionary flow, a vital *transfiguration* occurs in the way we regard our bodily identities. Instead of thinking of these identities as conventionally discrete numerical or geometrical mathematical 'figures', that is as concrete 'statistics on a government chart' pushed or pulled around by local force, we can reclaim our unique personhood that comes *through* our dynamic locality as inclusions of energy flow. We open up our 'I' self to the inclusion of all around that flows into and out from us as breathing holes in the flow, receptive to, protective of and responsive to our ever-changing natural neighbourhood. As we do this, maybe we will also recognize the need for our conventional discontinuous logical and mathematical foundation to transfigure.

'Honeysuckle Sharing Circle' (Oil painting on canvas by Alan Rayner, 2003). *The painting is centred around a candelabra of honeysuckle blooms. Each bloom is unique in its own sweet way and at a different stage of development – some unopened, some freshly bursting, others yellowing. The blooms face outwards in a representation of combined receptivity and responsiveness towards an inward facing fringe of other flowers, interleaved with grasses: white rockrose; red campion; orange hawkweed; yellow-wort; green hellebore; bluebell; a mystery plant (actually an artistically licensed version of woad,*

original source of indigotine); violet. The stalk of the honeysuckle winds spirally outwards and then back inwards and downwards to its self origin, creating a pool of reflection, black in the middle and transforming through shades of blue to silver around its outside. When no thing comes between, then no thing pools together a diversity of inner self with outer self-domains, waving correspondence through complementary relationship of one with another, embodying light with shadow across the spectrum of possibilities in common space.

4. Fluidity as Tolerance

Creative Intention

Here I offer an appreciation of fluid tolerance as vital to evolutionary creativity, not just as an aid to putting up with difference. Along the way I offer some insights about the fundamental nature of ecological and evolutionary sustainability and its sociological implications.

What on Earth is Sustainable?

A good question to ask
When all that's given
Of incomparable value
Seems to come at a price
Worth more or worth less
As a set of commodities
On the supermarket shelf
Of vacuum-packaged distress

Where what scores most regularly
Is considered most consistently
To be the best
Of those put to the test
To be singled out
For maximum uniform production
Of an elite order
And preserved in a perpetual pickle

Whilst discarding the rest
Of rampant variety
Into a stultifying space
Of squandered vitality

Placed under arrest
Somewhere else
Nowhere
Where none can have grace
To give of their best
What they gratefully receive

Meanwhile, as our favourite selection reigns supreme
It closes its hatches
Against all oddness
In a harrowing victory
That spells desolation
For each and all
In a row standing stiffly on proud parade
Amidst the fallen rank and filed
Away for safe keeping

Because no one kind
Can sustain itself
As a monoclonal antibody
Of corporate ill health
In narrowing arteries
Blocking the flow
Betwixt heart and head

What is truly downright ugly
In the natural world
Is the clot in the landscape
That claims for itself
All credit for wealth

Of human despair crying
Never heard but trying
Itself to the limit

Within drab straight walls
That shut out the wildness
That burns to come in

A wildness whose life cannot deaden
And whose death can only enliven
The vital space
Breathing in and out
The fresh air and water
Flowing through channels
Of pulsating arteries
Sustaining supply from a pool
That empties as it fills
With no fear of drought
Or stagnant disgrace

Rich in expression
Of rampant variety
Through irregular heartbeat
Of present giving what passes
Through central reception
Into continual future

Where all that can be sustained
Are sustained
Accepting the invitation
To hold, protect and pass on
The capacity to flourish
In a pool that ripples and ruffles
Amid spells of calm

To ask what on Earth is sustainable
Is not the same
As to ask what's best

To preserve in isolation
As a keeper of deadness

But to ask what can keep going
By giving what's given
Its unique evanescence
To sustain the flow
Of what's coming around
In perishable packaging
To have not to hold
For ever

'I'm Migration' (Oil painting on canvas by Alan Rayner, 1999). *Implicit in the outward forms of migrant birds and animals are travellers' tales of flights and treks, of arrivals, departures and time in motion. The migrants bring with them a cultural heritage that enriches the lives of residents. In its long journey, an English Swallow, dark from above, light from below, swallows landscape. Its travail begins in the elemental South African solar heat that is transformed by photosynthesis into protea flowers. The heat generates a propelling force that*

carries the bird over veldt, above water-seeking springboks, across deserted sand dunes and dark-light realms of fluttering hoopoes until green-topped, white cliffs signal arrival time before May begins to bloom. Speedwell urges onwards; forget-me-not reminds of home; cowslips reflect the strengthening warmth of rising sun, and terns join in aerobatic arrival celebrations. But where is the welcome for human immigrants? Nothing reinforces cancerous invasive potential more strongly than the alienation of the new arrival, one way or the other.

Tolerance: How Inclusional Awareness Can Unblock the Flow of Human Understanding

Drawing Lines – The Mythical Grounds for Objective Intolerance

That's the limit! You've got to draw the line somewhere!

How often do we come across such expressions and how often do we use them ourselves? What do they reveal about our thinking and feeling?

Most fundamentally, these expressions say something profound about how many of us have come to view both nature and human nature as realms of fearful possibility that must be contained within acceptable bounds if we are to establish any kind of order to our lives that will enable us to settle down and/or make progress. As Robert Frost put it –

Nature does not complete things. She is chaotic. Man must finish, and he does so by making a garden and building a wall.

In other words, these expressions signify judgmental attitudes of intolerance towards anything outside our comfort zone that we deem to be unacceptable or downright 'wrong'. Oddly, we – by which I mean 'many of us' – can take great pride in these attitudes as our way of making the world a better place and one another better people, forging ahead in an ongoing battle of good versus evil, positive against negative, light against darkness, order against chaos, wisdom against stupidity, civilization against wildness, beauty against ugliness, health against disease, etc. We tell ourselves mythical stories about this battle and erect symbolic monuments to celebrate the lives and deaths of those who have won great victories or fallen gloriously in the cause of one against other. We fill the schoolbooks of our children with ticks and crosses so that they can be certain in the knowledge of what's right and what's wrong. We reward those who tick our boxes whilst meting out punishment to those who don't meet the standard criteria we lay down for what's acceptable. We make it harder and harder not to conform and strike out in new directions from what has gone before.

Underlying these outward expressions of intolerance is a whole system of restrictive logic that has become deeply embedded, over thousands of years, in the foundations of our language, mathematics, science, theology and governance. This is the definitive logic of objective rationality, whose foundations are grounded in a declaration of the independent exclusivity of one thing from every other thing, otherwise known as 'the law of the excluded middle'. By absolute definition, this law has zero tolerance for any form of thinking in which one thing simultaneously includes and is included in another thing. Only the positivistic and dialectic logics respectively of 'one or other' or 'both one and the other in mutually contradictory apartheid' are permitted, and neither of these logics can tolerate the other.

The most fundamental basis for this logic of intolerance is an absolute dichotomy between two kinds of universal presence, 'material' and 'immaterial', such that the latter is treated as a passive physical absence ('nothing') and the former as an active and reactive physical presence ('something'). From this dichotomy, other definitive divisions arise, for example between animate and inanimate, mind and matter, God and Nature, organism and environment, masculine and feminine, order and disorder, positive and negative, etc.

A few moments' reflection reveals that this dichotomy does not and cannot make sense, because a purely immaterial entity would be featureless void, whereas a purely material one would be a dimensionless concrete point. In an observably featured, fluidly dynamic cosmos, material and immaterial presence can only be mutually inclusive, not mutually exclusive. Nature can only be a continuous energy flow of dynamic relational 'place-time', not a split field of discretely objectified matter and space motivated from somewhere ineffable. Matter cannot occupy or impose discrete limits upon space because space permeates matter.

Although this dichotomy doesn't make sense and fails to take account either of our actual human living and dying experience or evidence implicit in modern scientific theories of relativity, quantum mechanics and non-linear dynamical systems, it is still taken for granted and taught as the basis for all rigorous analysis and problem-solving to this day. The dimensionless concrete point mass remains the starting point for all orthodox mathematics. This point underpins the discontinuity of finite material figures from their non-finite spatial background in the arithmetic of discrete numbers and the abstract Euclidian and non-Euclidian geometries that conflate space with a three-dimensional cube or curved surface. How on Earth should we have become so dependent on such abstract nonsense – and is it really as good for us as we lead ourselves to believe every day in every way in almost everything we say and do as educators, politicians, philosophers, scientists, technologists, clerics, managers and advertising executives?

Fear of 'Something Wrong': The Paradoxical Breeding Ground for Intolerant Attitude

Somehow we seem to have made a virtue of intolerant logic as the very grounds upon which we base our enquiries and explanations of nature and human nature. But, wait a minute, don't many of us also think there's something 'wrong' with 'intolerance', some kind of rigid inflexibility that stifles our own and others' creative potential and ability to attune with changing circumstances, whilst bringing us inevitably into conflict with whatever or whoever doesn't agree with us? How is it possible to be gentle and compassionate in our relationships with those in our neighbourhood if we cannot tolerate their presence and actions? The enigma is eloquently summarized by Shakespeare's Hamlet:

> To be or not to be, that is the question: whether 'tis nobler in the mind to suffer the slings and arrows of outrageous fortune, or to take arms against a sea of troubles, and by opposing end them?

Such is the paradox that has been built into the foundations of human thought for millennia through the mental dislocation of matter from space – that we preach the virtues of tolerance at the same time as fearing it will expose us individually and/or collectively to enfeeblement and evil forces. Clearly, somewhere along the line, this paradox arises from the idea that there is something intrinsically *bad* about nature and human nature, which must be kept in check. That we should be capable of having such an idea makes our addiction to objective rationality understandable psychologically, despite the philosophical and scientific irrationality of its abstract exclusion of immaterial presence.

What makes us believe that there is necessarily anything *bad* about what brought us into the world in the first place? To believe this is like railing against our Mother, complaining that we never asked to be born. In the process, we become alienated from nature, desiring to define and eliminate all that's imperfect about it, so as to ensure a pain-free, immortal existence of endless bliss, if not here on Earth, then somewhere else. In that alienation may lie the true story of the Fall, our mythical expulsion from the

Garden of Earthly Delights and ensuing insatiable quest for perfect purity that we imagine will somehow allow us to regain our lost Paradise. The logical conclusion of such a quest for purity can, however, only be stasis, not a vibrant life full of passion, but an encapsulation in virus-like Platonic ideal forms of frozen geometry.

It seems all too obvious that what makes us believe something's wrong with our natural origins is the undeniable reality that, as local individual identities, we can suffer and die. We want to free ourselves from that reality and so seek to perfect some form of invulnerable existence that excludes us from it. Our intolerance of painful reality sets in train a desire for exclusivity that alienates 'self' and 'us' from 'other', enabling us ultimately to live paradoxically as if we are independent entities – exceptions from a Nature that in reality can make no exceptions. This desire becomes embedded in the foundations of a logic that tolerates no weakness – a logic that expresses itself in the Darwinian terms of 'survival of the fittest'. We come to perceive ourselves and other life forms as independent 'survival machines', competing for superiority, with no room for compassionate fellow feeling in a 'dog eats dog' culture.

I remember when I was a child I hated being ill, not so much because of the suffering, which could always be soothed by tender loving care, but because my parents said it was because there was something *wrong with me*. I took this literally to mean that somehow my illnesses, of which I had many, were *my own fault*, so that they became a continual source of guilt and shame, a double curse. When I was ill or injured, I wanted to hide away somewhere where no one could see the dreadful evidence of my failure.

When my mother was dying and I had to tell my ancient father that I needed to take him from his hospital bed to see her urgently, he asked, 'What's wrong with her then?' Later, as I watched tears flowing down my father's face whilst he held my mother's hand when a nurse told him that she had passed away, I wondered what solace this perception that she had died because there was something wrong with her could bring to him.

What if what's actually wrong is this very perception of what's wrong that leads us to regard ourselves as not good enough survival machines in need of improvement? What if whatever makes us individually vulnerable is actually vital to our collective ability to live, love and evolve in co-creative dynamic relationship? What then, would be the human cost of seeking material perfection and enshrining this as a condition for individual approval?

The Tolerance of Natural Variability in the Evolutionary Flow of 'Place-Time'

As a keen observer of nature, Charles Darwin was struck by the extraordinary natural variability of life forms. For good reason, he saw this variability as vital for the evolution of diverse species. But he invented a mechanism to bring about this evolution that is perversely intolerant of variety, namely 'natural' selection as 'the preservation of favoured races in the struggle for life'.

Implicit in this idea of selection is the notion that natural variability arises as a set of noisy deviations from an optimal standard, which can be weeded out progressively until only the most competitively exclusive remains. It is clearly underpinned by a perception of 'something wrong' with natural variability, which is sorted out by the imposition of a death penalty on all those most vulnerable and so not good enough to succeed in gaining the favour of a forceful judgmental authority. The linkage of such perceptions to the intolerance of objective rationality and its manifestation in a huge variety of abusive human behaviours, from setting one another 'exams' to genocide and world war is also clear.

But what if natural variability was understood not as a basis for competing in gladiatorial combat to see which discrete individual entities are most fit to occupy a fixed arena, but instead as an expression of the tolerant room for possibility vital for evolutionary co-creativity with an ever-changing environmental context? Not only might we be more able to tolerate one another's idiosyncrasies and vulnerabilities, but we could recognize that these latter actually sustain the tolerance of natural fluid flow, which enables local obstructions to be dislodged, transformed and circumvented. When we contemplate, for example, the swirling flows of rivers, oceans, atmospheres and galaxies, we cannot fail to notice the endless variety of evanescent appearances that, like our individual selves, emerge and submerge as distinct but not discrete local expressions of currents that can have no discrete beginnings or endings. If we were to single out and reproduce only particular variants as examples of 'best practice', what kind of flow could they add up to?

To gain this understanding requires, however, a much deeper understanding of the real meaning and origins of tolerance as a vital quality of all nature as a continuous energy flow that includes human beings. It involves much, much more than just passively putting up with what we as individuals might regard as a 'necessary evil', which simply perpetuates the idea of something wrong with nature and human nature. It requires the reclamation of what objective rationality has alienated from its exclusive logic as a source of vulnerability and uncertainty, but which is also vital to the flow of evolutionary creativity: the receptive omnipresence of space everywhere as a dynamic inclusion of matter in the continuous 'place-time' of natural energy flow.

Tolerance cannot remove suffering because it naturally entails suffering. But with its deeper understanding comes recognition that what brings suffering also brings the life and love in which our individual lives and deaths are naturally included not as extinguishable objects but as dynamic relational flow-forms in continuous communion. We can come to understand the vital contribution of our individual natural inclusion in an evolutionary process of co-creative, fluid dynamic transformation of all through all in receptive spatial context. This is no monotonous solo 'survival of the fittest' in splendid isolation, but a continually improvising orchestration of many-voiced harmonies ensuring the 'sustainability of the fitting'. Evolutionary creativity doesn't naturally perfect isolated individuals – it sustains their dynamic relationship in an ongoing relay of receiving and passing on.

Opening Channels
With deep tolerance comes the possibility of transforming the 'dead line' that isolates one thing exclusively from another into a vibrant communication channel of each including other in the continuous flow of many that includes one and one that includes many in dynamic relationship. Here, there is nothing fundamentally wrong with nature or human nature that needs to be excluded or can be excluded, because nature does not and cannot make exceptions from the receptive influence of space everywhere. But intolerance of this reality can, in the long run, only compound, not end suffering, through the opposition of one against other that naturally include one another in the evolutionary communion of their common space. It is our rationalistic intolerance of immaterial presence, not what we might call the sea of troubles, which needs to loosen up if we are to get out of the fix that draws us into civil war with our natural neighbourhood.

Making Allowances for Evolutionary Creativity: The Autocatalytic Influence of Receptive Space

From Restrictive Imposition to Receptive Invitation – The Deletion and Induction of Natural Variation

Even some of its strong advocates have recognized a profound logical difficulty with Darwin's concept of 'natural selection' as 'the preservation of favoured races in the struggle for life', in that such a restrictive mechanism cannot in itself be evolutionarily creative (e.g. Briggs and Walters, 1984; Rayner, 1997). This fundamental difficulty has, however, neither prevented the almost complete acceptance of the concept within the biological sciences nor the extension of its underlying principles throughout all kinds of academic discipline, economic and social governance, educational curricula and peer review systems based on the rationalization of natural energy flow into discrete units. With the added impetus provided by selfish gene theory (Dawkins 1989) and sociobiology (Wilson, 1998) there has been an increasing tendency to perceive and manage people and organisms simplistically *as if* they truly are competitive survival machines (Curtis 2007). In this process, it may well be that what is truly vital to human and natural creativity is being suppressed and neglected, resulting in deep misunderstanding, environmental damage, human distress and conflict (Rayner 2003, 2004).

As an ecological resolution of this difficulty, Rayner (1997) suggested the need for a fluid dynamic concept of 'niche' as what he then called a 'selection vacuum' or 'opportunity space', which induces continual evolutionary transformation. Here, environment and organism continually and inseparably include and shape one another as outer context and inner content of the same variably resistive dynamic system or energy flow, in much the same way that landscape features simultaneously shape and are shaped by the erosive flow of a river. The flow of informational content in the system itself is made possible and locally reduces and increases resistance through the opening up and reinforcement of spatial channels for further flow in an autocatalytic process of change begetting change. The evolution of a tree creates an opportunity for a climbing plant. The accumulation of sand by annual plants at the front of a sand dune system creates an opportunity for a succession of perennial plant communities and associated animals, fungi and micro-organisms to establish and follow in one another's wakes, culminating in forest. Earth's biosphere expands out from oceans to land and sky – and from microbes to people capable of venturing beyond the immediate confines of the planet's atmosphere.

Instead of a rigidly prescriptive process in which individuals or their genes as objectively discrete units of selection are forced to fit or adapt to the constraints of predetermined environmental settings or 'end goals', a co-creative, improvisational, dynamic relationship occurs between content and context. Indeed the 'content' is 'contextual', i.e. an inseparable dynamic inclusion of the 'context' like a river in its basin, a river basin in a landscape, a tree in a forest, a forest in biosphere, a biosphere in cosmos, without ultimate limit. Each reconfigures in *complementary*, simultaneously receptive and responsive dynamic relationship with the influence of the other. Correspondingly, each by *making allowances* as a dynamic inclusion of the same, variably resistive but continuous energy flow *inductively* invites the other to transform in a richly creative and ultimately unpredictable dance. This interplay continually adds new variations on an evolving theme that includes all simultaneously responding receptively to all in what can become an extremely complex and diverse communion, albeit one based on very simple fluid dynamic principles. It is quite unlike the predictable linear progression of conventional evolutionary theory, which grinds towards a singular fixed end on what has been called an 'adaptive peak' through one *forcefully* restricting the expression of the other until all possibilities for diversity and innovation are competitively excluded (e.g. Futuyma, 1986).

Dynamic Boundaries

For the creative interplay just described to be possible, the informational interfacings or dynamic relational boundaries of all forms of living organization themselves have to be fluid and hence indeterminate to varying degrees, not absolutely rigid and sealed. This variable fluidity allows them to attune in an energetically sustainable way with heterogeneous local conditions within the common space of their ultimately limitless natural neighbourhood. Under energy-rich conditions ('abundance'), processes of 'self-differentiation' bring about the proliferation of relatively permeable, deformable informational boundaries in highly branched or subdivided formations. Under conditions of energy shortage ('scarcity'), processes of 'self-integration' minimize boundary formation through processes of sealing, fusion and redistribution, which conserve and recycle energy in relatively undivided or networked survival, channelling and explorative structures. Examples of the reciprocal dynamic relationship between informational boundary differentiation and integration amongst organic forms of life on Earth can be found from molecular to ecosystem scales of organization, but are perhaps most explicit in the heterogeneous growth forms of fungi. The developmental versatility of indeterminate organization in fungal mycelia as they expand and encounter one another in spatially and temporally varying conditions of resource availability in their natural habitats has enabled some of them to attain vast sizes, measurable in square kilometres, and ages of thousands of years (Rayner, 1997).

The requisite changes in boundary fluidity that allow living systems to attune in an energetically sustainable way with their contextual circumstances can be brought about chemically, through shifts between 'primary' and 'secondary' metabolism in response to internal and external environmental reduction-oxidation potential. For example, the oxidative cross-linking of phenolic, terpenoid, proteinaceous and fatty compounds can harden and seal boundaries through the production of compounds like melanin, lignin, keratin, cutin and suberin. Such hardening and sealing of boundaries in response to the presence of oxygen in the gaseous phase, where molecules diffuse ten thousand times faster than through water, was vital to the emergence of terrestrial life forms, and further exemplifies how life catalyses its own evolution. Oxygen not only energizes organic life through its consumption during aerobic respiration, but has the potential to destroy the physical and chemical integrity of protoplasm through the production of reactive oxygen species and free radicals. This is due to its receptive spatial affinity for electrons, which it accepts one at a time in the course of its reduction to water. The liberation of oxygen into the atmosphere through photosynthesis was, therefore, perhaps the greatest challenge and opportunity that organic life on Earth has so far presented itself with in the course of its early evolution. Through the development of chemical means to incorporate the simultaneous threat and promise of oxygen into cycles of growth, death, decomposition and regeneration, life allowed itself hugely to amplify the diversity and scope of its transformation of predominantly solar energy into a myriad forms and processes (Rayner, 1997).

Through inhabiting dynamic interfacial boundaries that cannot absolutely isolate into *opposite* sides – they can only vary the resistance to communication between *complementary* insides and outsides – living systems can never form truly discrete, independent units. Any model of evolutionary process that depends on the selection or singling out of discrete units from their environmental context cannot, therefore, be truly representative of natural systems and may in some circumstances lead to profound misunderstanding (Rayner, 2000). So, what is the attraction of such models, and why do they persist?

Individualistic Perfectionism – The Self-preservation of a Fixed Idea
Psychological analysis of such discourse as 'selection', 'preservation of favoured races in the struggle for life', 'survival of the fittest', 'competitive exclusion', 'selfish genes' and 'survival

machines' reveals all the hallmarks of obsession with some kind of 'ideal being' or 'chosen one' that doesn't perish. This obsession has been evident throughout recorded human history, associated with notions of sovereignty and hierarchical structure founded on systems of rationalistic logic that divide and close off one kind of existence from another. These systems are deeply embedded in orthodox mathematics, language, science, theology and governance.

It serves the interests of this obsession to deny or exclude any kind of natural influence or presence that could erode the boundaries of permanent structure. Battle lines are drawn that oppose the 'forces' of 'order', 'light' and 'right' with the 'forces' of 'chaos', 'darkness' and 'wrong'. 'Positive' is singled out as 'good', which sustains material being, whilst 'negative' is singled out as 'bad', which takes away from definitive existence. 'Male' comes to symbolize 'positive', whilst 'female' symbolizes 'negative'. The quest to preserve 'good' becomes an ongoing struggle against the 'enemy' of 'entropy'. 'Sacred' geometries of 'perfectly' closed, symmetrical, crystalline forms are idealized as eternal time capsules. Man declares war on nature and his own nature, seeking to remove whatever makes him perishable. But in so doing, he tries to manufacture a paradoxical reality in which matter is independent from space, capable of evolving in its own right, by force either of its internal will or an external executive agency, an unmoved mover of the kind envisaged by Aristotle, which can move others without moving itself.

Clearly, there is no room when under the spell of this obsession to make allowances for what makes the allowances needed for evolutionary fluidity and co-creativity. There is no room to include the receptive immaterial presence of space everywhere in the absolute Whole of One Alone, whether this is a three-dimensional Euclidian Cube extended to infinity, or the 'finite but unbounded' depthless curved surface of conventional non-Euclidian geometries. The 'wholes' and 'parts', the 'one' and 'many' of rationalistic 'holism' and 'reductionism' are excluded from one another by the 'either/or', or 'both-and in mutual apartheid' unrealistic logical dichotomies of one-sided positivism and pluralistic dialectics. There is no room for consideration of the vital involvement of receptive space in natural energy flow, which eases the passage for responsive and hence necessarily unfixed structure to reconfigure into endless variety. Instead this flow is simplistically reduced from a dynamic relational *flow of space* – that is as a mutual dynamic embodiment of responsive, resistive informational and receptive, yielding spatial phases in a continuously transforming stream – to an atomized *flow through space* as a stream of discontinuous material entities.

Inclusional Neighbourhood – The Autocatalytic Influence of Receptive Space

Once stuck in the rut of simplistic definition, which sacrifices truth for the sake of linguistic and arithmetical convenience and a false sense of security and freedom, it can be difficult to get out, for both psychological and pragmatic if not good scientific reasons. But no sooner is the inductive role of receptive space admitted – or re-admitted – into our understanding of dynamic material form, then paths of least resistance open up that allow everything, literally, to flow thermally and gravitationally into continually transforming place. Life doesn't just follow pre-existing paths of least resistance, life creates them and in the process catalyses its own creativity without need for either an internal or external executive force. All becomes understandable in terms of inductive influence, not forceful imposition.

The 'unmoved mover' of Nature is correspondingly not to be found in an executive material agency that acts upon reactive others according to Newton's Laws of Motion, some mystical One Alone figure, which can move the Earth given a long enough lever and somewhere to stand on. But she may be found in the immaterial presence of material absence everywhere that allows the possibility of responsive relationship. She can be heard in silence and seen in darkness and felt in the pit of the stomach, cold sweat and the cockles of the heart, not the shake, rattle and flash of forceful explosion that is drawn into her bodily manifestation. Her influence is implosive, not explosive, and without it no life or death or love or hate or movement or warmth or echo or creativity or destruction is possible. She may have been alluded to in many names, Tao, Buddha Nature, Holy Ghost, Brahman, Kali, Wakan-Tanka, Great Spirit etc, and found in many places, including the corrosive and dissolving presences of oxygen and water, but few perhaps have truly recognized her for what she both is and is not.

The dynamic inclusion of receptive space in natural fluid flow is the basis for the 'logic of the including middle' or 'inclusionality', which has the effect of transforming the rigid intolerance of objective rationality into a much more permissive and creative view of life and evolutionary process. This receptive space is what Rayner (1997) initially referred to as 'selection vacuum' and 'dynamic niche', but has now incorporated into the concept of 'natural inclusion' as 'the fluid dynamic, co-creative, transformation of all through all in receptive spatial context' (Rayner, 2006, 2008). Natural inclusion correspondingly shifts the spotlight of 'natural selection' from its focus on the one-way adaptation of discrete individuals or groups to an objectively prescriptive set of external conditions through a process of competitive narrowing down, to a multi-way dynamic relational attunement of each with other in continually co-creative flow. The perfection of individual survival machines in competition with one another is not only incompatible with such flow, it is impossible and meaningless, for what is energetically sustainable in this context is continually changing. Perfection is not a quantifiable property of discrete, self-centred entities; it is a quality of harmonious dynamic relationship that cannot be sustained without involvement of the receptive space that allows boundaries both to perish and reconfigure within its inductive, autocatalytic influence.

With the recognition that it is dynamic spatial relationship, not individual autonomy that is important to the creativity and sustainability of evolutionary processes, a very different appreciation of the true nature of self-identity emerges. Instead of being a purely intrinsic, definable possession of discrete individuals independent from their environmental context, *self identifies with neighbourhood* as a dynamic, co-creative inclusion of one within other. Instead of being regarded as separators of one from another, the bodily boundaries of living organisms and organizations are understood to be dynamic informational interfacings that simultaneously outline inner world and inline outer world as distinct but not discrete contributors to the same complex self-identity (Rayner, 2004). The boundaries become inclusive, not exclusive middles, joins that make allowances not excisions, through the distinction but not isolation of one in another.

Acknowledgement of interdependence thereby supersedes declarations of independence, so that loving care for natural neighbourhood no longer seems an irrational negation of genetic survival needs, but makes common sense as a vital inclusion of sustainable self-identity. The very basis for conflict, as a product of opposition between one and other, is removed as the loving influence of receptive space is restored to primacy, not as sickly sentimentality but the very heart of what it means to be truly human and natural, deeply painful as it is to admit the individual vulnerability that this necessarily entails. This is not to say that individuals can't or shouldn't express aggressive, resistive and protective patterns of behaviour, since these are vital to the differentiation and sustainability of natural diversity. But it is to say that these expressions should not be regarded as the inevitable product of enmity between independent beings striving to gain from one another's annihilation.

Inclusional Catalysis: From Forced Fit to Induced Fitting

It has long been recognized that the chemical transformations needed to sustain organic life on Earth would be impossibly slow without the assistance of these transformations' own catalysts – enzymes. Enzymes are proteins that catalyze not only such fundamental processes as respiration and photosynthesis, but also their own synthesis via their dynamic informational relationship with the 'genetic code' contained in the sequence of triplets of purine and pyrimidine bases along the length of molecules of deoxyribonucleic acid and ribonucleic acid (DNA and RNA). The importance of receptive space in this dynamic relationship in many ways epitomizes the co-creative synergism between content and context, and between differentiation and integration that is expressed in diverse ways and at different scales throughout nature. First of all there is extremely close correspondence between the way the genetic code specifies particular kinds of amino acids and the way these amino acids relate spatially with one another in proteins such that the latter function optimally as catalysts. Secondly, this function is dependent on the configuration of what is known as the 'active site' of enzymes but might more aptly be called the *receptive space* where chemical compounds known as 'substrates' are brought into correspondence in such a way as to facilitate their association and dissociation with and from one another to form 'products'.

For a long while, the relationship between enzyme and substrate was thought about rationalistically in much the same way as niche and organism, that is, as 'lock' and 'key'. For the key to operate the lock, it had to fit precisely the prescriptive specifications of the active site of the lock, as defined by the informational structure of the protein, which is defined in turn by the sequence of amino acids which is defined by the sequence of bases in DNA and/or RNA. Studies of the actual dynamics of enzyme catalysis eventually showed, however, that this highly restrictive, hard-line mechanism is inadequate to account for observation, and a more fluid, dynamic relational process is involved, known as 'induced fit'. Here enzyme and substrate make allowances for inclusion of and by the other, through changes in their spatial configuration.

The transformation from 'natural selection' to 'natural inclusion' as a basis for understanding evolutionary process in many ways involves relaxation from a rigidly objective lock and key model to a more accommodating 'induced fitting' relationship between organism and environment in which each dynamically includes the other. Instead of randomly generating a set of independently variable genetic 'keys' that are individually tested for their ability to meet environmental specifications, and discarding those that do worst in favour of those that do best, there is opportunity for 'content' to co-evolve with 'context' in mutual dynamic relationship.

Such a transformation might not only help us to deepen and enrich our understanding of how the 'Law of the Jungle' continually reconfigures its evolutionary boundaries instead of setting them in concrete. It could also help us to relax the creativity-stifling, pain-aggravating definitions we are prone continually to impose on human individuals and social formations, through adherence to rationalistic standards of judgment.

Encouraging Co-creativity by Making Allowances in Human Organizations

The occurrence of restrictive practices based on definitive theory is evident throughout modern human culture and organizations. The rules and regulations of structures and strictures that impose unnaturally discrete limits on natural energy flow abound. In many ways we have allowed ourselves to become driven by abstraction of matter from space into conformity with time schedules, job descriptions, action plans, legal constraints, educational curricula, financial imperatives, administrative boundaries and hierarchies etc, that force us to become deeply alienated from one another and our natural neighbourhood. This alienation disrupts our improvisational ability to attune harmoniously with changing contextual circumstances, which is the essence of ecological and evolutionary sustainability and creativity. It renders our inapt self-definition as competitive survival machines into self-fulfilling prophecy, a dystopia of psychological, social and environmental abuse and devastation, lacking any kind of natural coherence or kindness that enables us simply to live, love and be loved, in reasonable comfort and with sufficient stimulation to keep our minds and muscles active.

But there is no obligation for us to live in this unsustainable way of forced fitness – indeed there is every requirement for us to stop teaching ourselves to do so if there is to be hope for the evolutionary sustainability of humanity in the long run. We can instead learn, or re-learn, the improvisational ways of 'induced fitting' through co-creatively making mutually encouraging allowances that come from accepting and acknowledging the diversity of our natural inclusion in receptive spatial context. As these ways are brought increasingly into dynamically receptive and responsive forms of human organization and truly educational practice, so too can increase the possibility of living enjoyable, caring and fruitful lives, freed from self-inflicted poverty, addiction, conflict and oppression. But for this possibility to be realized, we have to give up the quest for the holy grail of self-preservation, which holds us to ransom in paradoxically seeking individual perfection as autonomous beings in an inescapably variable and unpredictable energy flow. This flow can never be an eternally level playing field for us to compete to be best on, until and unless all warmth is withdrawn and what some may imagine to be Hell freezes over. Then we really will have succeeded in being preserved forever in crystalline geometry, running on the spot like frantic Red Queens atop adaptive peaks of most fit, not most fitting through making allowances in dynamic relationship!

'Loving Error' (Oil painting on board by Alan Rayner, 1998). *This painting illustrates the dynamic interplay between differentiation and integration, irregularity ('error') and regularity, and negative draining and positive outpouring that is embedded in living system boundaries. The erratic fire in the venation of a lobed ivy leaf is bathed in the integrating embrace of a heart-shaped leaf which converts negative blue and mauve into positive scarlet and crimson. The midrib of the heart-shaped leaf emerges as a bindweed which communicates between extremes of coldness and dryness.*

5. Creativity at Heart

Creative Intention
Here I inquire into the deep origins of human creativity within natural creativity.

> ### The Hole in the Mole
> *I AM the hole*
> *That lives in a mole*
> *That induces the mole*
> *To dig the hole*
> *That moves the mole*
> *Through the earth*
> *That forms a hill*
> *That becomes a mountain*
> *That reaches to sky*
> *That connects with stars*
> *And brings the rain*
> *That the mountain collects*
> *Into streams and rivers*
> *That moisten the earth*
> *That grows the grass*
> *That freshens the air*
> *That condenses to rain*
> *That carries the water*
> *That brings the mole*
> *To Life*

'The Hole in the Mole' (Oil painting on canvas, by Alan Rayner, 2001).

The Sexual Cosmos – Where Creativity Really Comes From in the Inclusional Flow of Open Space

Pregnant Pause

Adults often laugh when their offspring carry on as if they've just invented sex. Perhaps the cosmos laughs in the same way when biological scientists seriously contemplate how sex might have evolved, and what its implications are for the survival prospects of selfish genes. Could anything be more ridiculous? What planet do they think they are on? How on Earth could anything, let alone a selfish gene, come into being without the receptive darkness that brings love to life in light? But so neglectful and fearful of spatial receptivity has our do-it-yourself positivistic culture become that any consideration of what Lao Tzu called 'the mysterious valley' is rejected beyond the bounds of material definition and we are left wondering how concrete makes love! And light, the truly inexplicable, is left to co-create nature on its own, whilst darkness looks on impassively.

Where Not to Start – At the Point of No Return
The trouble begins at that very moment when we assume that anything has to begin at a certain point in time, as if it must either be a fully-fledged cosmic chicken or a newly-laid cosmic egg with no prior history – a 'magical something out of nothing'. Within this point lies the deepest superstition embedded within so-called 'rational' and 'objective' thought, a paradoxical, dimensionless 'peg' on which to hang the Emperor's hard-lined clothes that cover up his vulnerable birthday suit.

Here is where any rationalist can be found wanting, no matter how much he may protest the sound reason and hard evidence on which his case for the prosecution of the spirit is founded – for the reason is paradoxical and the evidence a convenient figment of imagination that obscures truth and suits his objective purpose. Any child who hasn't been caught in his spell can point this out, by drawing attention to the fact that it doesn't make sense to dissociate the infinite 'openness' of 'space' from the finite 'substantiality' of matter in a world of energy flow that doesn't stand still forever. A purely material world, without space, would indeed be a dimensionless, lifeless 'point', a discontinuity or singularity of the kind Euclid used magically to construct his abstract, three-dimensionally boxed geometry of width-less lines, depthless planes and space-cornering solids. A world of pure space would be featureless void, the very thought that scares the life out of rigidly imposed structure. The 'real world', as far as our human consciousness can allow us to discern, is neither dimensionless nor void, but is continually in flux, as Heraclitus recognized long before others insisted on confining it within fixed frameworks, the magical boxes that breed illusions of absolute individual freedom and collective security.

So, the trouble begins with what can only be regarded as an act of misogyny of the deepest kind – the declaration of a war of independence from the receptive space that permeates and eases the passage of all. From here on, life becomes 'a struggle for existence' in opposition to the continual threat of annihilation by 'other', now perceived at best as 'devouring mother'. Nature is said to 'abhor a vacuum', as if space had no place in her creative heart. Hamlet reflects on the threshold of his human tragedy:

*To be **or** not to be, that is the question: whether 'tis nobler in the mind to suffer the slings and arrows of outrageous fortune, **or to take arms against a sea of troubles**, and by **opposing end** them?*

The opposition of one against other, is eloquently depicted in the following excerpt from C.S. Lewis's 'Screwtape Letters' from a senior to an apprentice devil:

*The **whole** philosophy of Hell rests on a recognition of the axiom **that one thing is not another thing**, and, specifically, **that one self is not another self**. My good is my good and your good is yours. What one gains another loses. Even an inanimate object is what it is by excluding all other objects from the space it occupies; as it expands, it does so by pushing all other objects aside or by absorbing them. A self does the same... 'To be' means 'to be in competition'. Now the Enemy's philosophy is nothing more or less than one continued attempt to evade this very obvious truth. He aims at contradiction. Things are to be many, yet also one. The good of one self is to be the good of another. This impossibility he calls love, and this same monotonous panacea can be detected under all He does and* *even all He is – or claims to be. Thus He is not content, even Himself, to be a sheer arithmetical unity; He claims to be three as well as one, in order that this nonsense about Love may find a foothold in his own nature... The whole thing, in fact, turns out to be simply one more device for dragging in Love.*

The 'axiom that one thing is not another thing' is known as 'the Law of the Excluded Middle', which arises from the exclusion of space from matter that is embedded in the foundations of definitive logic upon which objective rationality depends. As Screwtape recognized, its very success depends on the divorce of reason from emotion that excludes the possibility of Love in a material, de-spirited cosmos, leaving us left to ponder one-sidedly on 'the evolutionary origin of sex'. How, then, could we humanly avoid being drawn into – and how might we release ourselves from – this rationalistic trap of the 'point of no return'. Perhaps the art will lie in discovering, within our hearts, the receptive space of 'the point of all return', the **turning point** that 'breathes love into light' through the dynamic inclusion of darkness.

The Mystery of Light as an Inclusion of Darkness in Natural Flow-Form

Although to a rationalistic mind, the notion of limitless space, perceived as infinite, indivisible void, may seem mysterious and decidedly inconvenient, perhaps the deeper mystery lies in understanding what comes naturally to configure this non-local omnipresence 'everywhere' into the locally unique expressions of natural flow-form of 'somewhere' distinctive. The latter 'informational' presence is what is vital, to paraphrase William Wordsworth, to render everything in natural energy flow distinct, yet nowhere defined into absolute, independent singleness. It is the very 'stuff' that materialists regard as 'all there is' to account for in a precise, demystified, quantitative depiction of the cosmos as an exact numerical system. Yet as soon as such accountancy imposes imaginary limits on the openness of space, the point of no return is reached where trouble and paradox begin.

In reality, we can only describe, we cannot explain this dynamic source of natural distinction: it just is as it is. But we can certainly misunderstand it profoundly by divorcing it from 'the love of darkness' that is a vital inclusion of its creative potential. This creative potential lies in an inexhaustible centre of continual renewal through the cycling and recycling of energy flow – what might justly be called the 'primordial womb of the cosmos', the receptive space that welcomes light into the dynamic correspondence that gives birth to natural flow-form. A centre distributed everywhere amongst dynamic localities that form in the hearts of every unique identity in the natural communion of one in all and all in one. A point of all return in an endless circulation, which transfigurally includes zero and infinity in its numbering of one and many, pooled together in receptive space. Where informational figure naturally includes spatial ground and spatial ground includes informational figure in the sensible, co-creative evolutionary relationships of a sexual cosmos, not the senseless alienation of independent sovereign states.

Five Pointers to the Point of All Return
1. Space, as limitless, eternal openness that cannot be cut, pervades matter/energy, not vice versa.
2. Regions of space free from matter/energy appear dark and feel intangible to sensors of all wavelengths (not just light visible to the naked eye) of electromagnetic radiation.
3. Matter/energy cannot exist independently from space, unless confined to an inert, dimensionless point.
4. All distinguishable (to our senses) form is local-in-nonlocal flow-form, a dynamic inclusion of space in matter/energy.
5. Time cannot exist independently from natural energy flow as a dynamic configuration of space.

Opening the Whole – *Intro-Ducing the Incorporate World of Inclusionality*

There seems to be a very widespread tendency amongst us human beings to view Nature and our Selves as if we consist of a complete set of 'Parts' and 'Wholes'. This has led to two alternative forms of philosophical and scientific enquiry into both Nature and Human Nature, which differ in whether they choose to focus on 'One' or 'Many' as their object(s) of selective attention. What has come to be called 'reductionism' seeks to differentiate 'One' into 'Many' fundamental or elementary constituent parts or particles, based on the supposition that once these latter are fully understood as independent 'building blocks', they can be re-assembled into a complete picture of the form and workings of what they were derived from. What has come to be called 'holism', on the other hand, seeks to understand the 'One' as an integral whole with 'emergent properties' beyond the sum of its parts due to the interconnectedness between these latter, which hence cannot be understood as fully independent entities. Correspondingly, we may view our individual selves either as 'one out of many isolated entities' – free but in competition with numerous others – or as 'part of a collective whole', like an interlocking piece of a jigsaw puzzle with a very particular space to occupy – secure alongside yet constrained by and set apart from the other pieces. In neither case is there any possibility for one to flow into or out from the other in mutual dynamic relationship.

This tendency has set the scene for a philosophical opposition between 'individual' or 'group', and 'one' or 'other', that has contributed to human conflict and environmental, social and psychological damage for millennia. Such opposition is evident throughout modern human life and culture. It underpins all scientific and religious beliefs in the existence of some internal or external executive 'force', which is enshrined in the definitive logic of the 'excluded middle' – the contention that 'one thing cannot simultaneously be another thing'. This premise of discontinuity is deeply embedded in the foundations of conventional mathematics, upon which rationalists seek to formalize the 'Laws of Nature' as unchanging rules that enable us to divide and predict the 'future' from the immediate 'past' – defined as a complete and prescriptive set of 'initial conditions'. It limits the creativity of all rationalistic systems of governance, education, research and personal decision-making and in spite of its intentions actually makes us *more* vulnerable to the *uncertain* influences that *invariably* get left out of the equations used to calculate our best laid plans. It leads us to speak of what 'drives' and 'determines' our behaviour and appearances, and to question how much this can be attributed to internal 'nature' ('genes') or external 'nurture' ('environment'), as if we could measure the contribution of a thrown stone and a pond to their mutual co-creation of a ripple. It makes us equate 'evolution' with 'natural' selection, what Darwin called 'the preservation of favoured races in the struggle for life' – an adversarial mechanism that in itself can, like cancer, only eliminate, not generate the 'diversity in community' of evolutionary life and Earthly ecosystems.

Such grounds for human conflict can never dissolve as long as we accept, without question, the validity of Hamlet's question:

To be or not to be, that is the question: whether 'tis nobler in the mind to suffer the slings and arrows of outrageous fortune, or to take arms against a sea of troubles, and by opposing end them?

Here, in stark relief, are etched the tragic implications of an attitude of mind that imposes discrete limits upon the provenances of 'one' and 'many' as opposing whole objects whose only alternative to existence is non-existence (annihilation or extinction). There is *no room* here, literally no *receptive* 'space' here, to accommodate the possibility of evolutionary flow of one into other because each is defined as a completely self-contained whole. One can thereby only be *entirely* subsumed into many and many can only be entirely subsumed into one through the loss of its or their capacity to vary their dynamic relational identity in correspondence with their neighbourhood. They can only be fit or not fit, not vary their fittingness as circumstances change.

But this *whole* story is obviously a fiction, premised on the notion that space – defined rationalistically as a void 'absence of material presence' or 'gap' – can be edged out from or edged into a *finite* location. In other words, the story is based on an absolute dichotomy between 'material' fixture, which constitutes 'something', and 'immaterial' void, which constitutes 'nothing'. For this to be true matter would have to exist *independently* from space and space would have to be *divisible* into discrete segments. But matter without space could only occupy a dimensionless point without size or shape (which is indeed the 'starting point' for deriving Euclid's 'idealized', three-dimensional geometry that draws a cubical box around infinity, as well as the so-called 'non-Euclidian' geometries that confine themselves to a depthless curved surface). And space alone would be formless, without any edge that could enable it to be cut into pieces, however subtle the knife one might try to apply. The inescapable conclusion is that material and immaterial are mutually inclusive finite and infinite presences, not mutually exclusive presence and absence. Moreover, in a cosmos that doesn't stand still forever and everywhere, receptive space is vital for the responsive movement of *fluid* material interfacing, not concrete material fixture, which gives it dynamic and varied local form as a natural energy flow.

So, what on Earth could have possessed us to try to place absolute limits on the inward and outward extent of discrete parts and wholes, allowing our lives to become so confined and driven by idealized – one might say idolized – concrete abstraction? It clearly cannot be something as sensible as rationalists assert and seem to believe. Maybe it has something to do with the way with the way we are predisposed cognitively to view and apprehend the world about us as omnivorous terrestrial primates with opposable thumbs and binocular eyesight. The latter help us to grasp and separate out things within a seemingly detached field of view that doesn't include ourselves as observers. Without pause for contemplation we may therefore overlook the fact that what we are looking out at actually includes us. Maybe the resulting illusory exemption of ourselves from our 'objective' field of view, which makes us feel fixed at the centre of our own universe, then gets reinforced by something more deeply psychological, like the fearful desire for self-preservation that associates with feeling threatened by the prospect of death, viewed as annihilation. If so, this truly is a fear to fear the utmost – the fear that seeks the refuge of certainty at all costs. It feeds its own suppositions by trying both logically and physically to wall out or wall in and so gain local dominion over the non-local, infinite omnipresence of material absence everywhere that cannot really be contained entirely within the whole or part of any structure as a fully definable entity. As Robert Frost put it:

> Nature does not complete things... Man must finish, and he does so by making a garden and building a wall.

This is the fear that fuels a vicious cycle of conflict between what is perceived as 'good' and 'bad' for self-preservation, a war of opposites between 'light' and 'darkness', 'male' and 'female', 'predator' and 'prey', 'strong' and 'weak'. It makes the objective perception of life as a loveless, cold-hearted 'struggle for existence' a self-fulfilling prophecy.

Something, or rather *somewhere vital* gets overlooked when striving to preserve life by encapsulating it, whether in some integral whole or in the set apart part that implies the existence of such a whole. What gets overlooked is that there can be no real life – only a suspended animation of the kind transiently present in dormant 'survival structures' like spores, cysts, seeds, bulbs, corms and hibernating animals – without opening up to the possibility of natural energy flow.

We cannot live without breathing. Yet in opening ourselves up to natural energy flow we also lose some of the local self-definition that would otherwise isolate our insides from our outsides as discrete objects. And with this loss, through which we gain life and a capacity for loving our neighbourhood as a vital inclusion of our self-identity, comes also the inevitability for us to suffer and perish in the short or long run as we take in and pass on energy supplies in an endless circulation. We *relay* energy through one to the other in a human race that is far from being naturally competitive or even co-operative, because its members are not and cannot be absolutely self-contained. We are neither absolutely divided off from one another nor from our environmental neighbourhood that sustains our dynamic local manifestation.

What is needed, therefore, to escape the confinement of whole and part that holds us to ransom, in opposition to one another and the world and cosmos about us, is a more naturally representative, fluid form of logic and geometry that opens our individual identity to the inclusion of neighbourhood in and as a vital aspect of self. Instead of envisaging ourselves as exceptions from or even as parts of Nature *as a whole*, there is a need for us to open up the imaginary boundary limits that we have been so prone to impose on existence, which deny our dynamic relationship with one another and Nature *as all*. Most fundamentally, we have to include the meaning of infinity and zero in our comprehension of the dynamic relational nature of 'self as neighbourhood'.

This 'opening of the whole', whether individual or group, to the infinite omnipresence of receptive space in natural energy flow is the basis for an understanding of nature and human nature that has been called 'inclusionality'. Inclusionality helps us to transform the 'whole' into a dynamic relational 'hole'. Hence we can understand the body of individual, world and cosmos as less like a rigid, bunged up bottle that preserves its contents forever, and more like a cup or grail with elastic walls, a dynamic natural inclusion of receptive space. This cup is like an open heart, a responsive receptacle that expands as it fills with and contracts as it circulates the life blood, the natural energy flow of its dynamic neighbourhood. With receptive space permeating everywhere, within, beyond and throughout its dynamic interfacial boundaries, it yields what it receives in equal measure in a natural *communion* of one in all and all in one, without end. In the words of John Lennon and Paul McCartney, the love it makes is equal to the love it takes, whether Christian, Jewish, Muslim, Buddhist, Taoist, Hindu, Pagan, Atheist or whatever else it might call itself. Far from being an exclusive corporate body, it is an incorporate body, truly spatially continuous and not just materially contiguous (interconnected) with its natural neighbourhood. It fluidly includes the *influence* of other in its self and the influence of its self in other's identity. Each is variably open to others' energetic influence. It has no need to oppose what ultimately and inescapably includes itself, open to endless creative evolutionary possibility.

What May Not Be Obvious
Every body is a cavity at heart
Every figure reconfigures both in science and in art
Every face is interfacing from no bottom to no top
Every faith is interfaith that cannot tell us where to stop
Every lining opens inwards as it brings its inside out
Every curtain closes outwards to conceal its inner doubt
Every story ends in opening from some future into past
Every glory is the story of finding first in last
Every aching is the making of another role for play
Every taking is the slaking of another's thirst to stay
Every tiding's no confiding with-out the trust to tell
Every siding is no hiding from the fear of utter Hell

Every flowing is the ebbing of another's world within
Every glowing is the lighting of the darkness in the spin
Every heartbeat is the murmur in the core of inner space
Every drumbeat is the echo of the dance within each place
Every silence is the gathering of the storm that is to come
When Love comes to Life

Your Welcome
I am here and there in everywhere
You are welcome
To where you find in me
That brings you peace and joy

But if you don't care
For what you find:
If my whispers make you shudder
Feeling lost without a rudder
Sending tingles down your spine
That make you clutch at straws
To keep yourself afloat
Struggling for survival
Against my infinite odds

Your welcome for me
To fill your heart
Will be non-existent
Your rage will be my sorrow
As you cling to thinking of tomorrow
Which is just another day
Like this one
Never ending

So, when I send my messenger
With open invitation

Be sure to know you're welcome
If only you can welcome
His care within your heart

Being Becoming Clear
I flow into Nature
As Nature flows into me
There In and Out There
Lives Our evolving identity
In gravitation's meeting with levitation
Where bodily soul and radiant spirit
Enfold that endless dark ground
Where neither meets with any resistance
But hold together in tension
What comes both before and after
In breathing envelope
That opens in closing
And closes in opening
Of morning in evening
And evening in morning

Passing on what enters in
In endless relay
Never lingering for an idol moment
Of Superstardom
Where light confines itself in itself
But has to find audience
In which to play
With the soul's delight
As day becomes night
And passes away
Into each breaking day

'Opening Endings' (Oil painting on canvas by Alan Rayner, 1999). *An elm tree's demise, its wing-barked boundaries opened by ravages of bark beetle and fungus, makes way for new life to fill its space. Maple leaves take over the canopy between earth and sky, but their coverage is only partial, leaving openings for arriving and departing flights of woodpeckers. Fungal decay softens the wood to allow the tunnelling of long-horn beetle larvae and probing and chiselling of beak-endings. A nest cavity provides a feeding station between egg and air.*

After Thought: The Flow-scape of the Mind and Co-creativity

We are air, water and land to which we will return.
We are the problem.
But we are also the solution.
I am better off, if you are better off [3]

Can we co-design systems and technologies that sustain a habitable future environment for us, or will we design systems that extract short term profits at the expense of **our future?**

If we accept that technology is design, then we have choices about what kind of technology can enable the planet to sustain us.

We could change our attitudes to people, animals and nature.

We could redesign democracy and governance so that each developed area has a sister area that they will support.

We could redesign the market to take social and economic considerations into account within an environmental context that can support future generations of life.

We could decide to tax pollution in the same way as we tax alcohol and other drugs, so as to encourage people to recognize its potential to harm our habitat.

We can exercise our freedom to create new ways of living and thinking to the extent that we afford the same freedom to others and respect our mutual human needs. In this way we can, without paradox, sustain our unique individual identities within the diverse collective communities that we both contribute to and receive from. In the core of our being is the imagination to create meaningful concepts. Alan Rayner inspires us to think about how we think about our natural communion and connection with all life forms. Now it is up to us:

A – Best Case Scenario: What an Inclusive, Co-creative Society Could be Like

We live in an environment that can support this and future generations.

Housing is affordable and made of sustainable materials. Clusters of homes share rain tanks and solar grids that are subsidised by local governments. Our living and working areas are powered by alternative energy. The new status symbol is the environmentally friendly lifestyle.

Public transport is green. Off-road vehicles are no longer permitted to private citizens. They can be hired for specific tasks and the kilometres are logged.

The green economy supports a vibrant job market spurred by subsidies to enable packaging goods, housing people, transporting people, educating and entertaining the public. The carbon economy is replaced through innovative inventions. All members of the public are encouraged to share their experiences and ideas for living sustainably. The futures market has been reconstructed to take into account the air, water and earth we need to grow organic, safe food.

People develop new economies and new trading systems that enable them to have time to enjoy many activities.

The clothes and shoes we wear are made of renewable resources. The windmill and fabric shoes are the new chic! People are mostly vegetarian because they understand that their carbon basket can be stretched further by growing their own veggies. Most waste is recycled locally and used for building or composting. Packaging is designed to ensure that waste is minimal.

Animals live in a carefully monitored environment to ensure *their* quality of life and ours. We are better off because we respect ourselves, one another (including sentient creatures) and the environment that includes us all. Bird flu, swine flu and bovine disease are unheard of in this scenario. We no longer take too many antibiotics, because we pause to recover from illnesses.

We live in harmony with the people of our region and our economy prospers through being able to work in one another's countries. We learn many languages. We are enriched by the diversity of language and culture. We are free and diverse in our neighbourhood, sub national region and super-national region, to the extent that our freedom does not undermine the freedoms of others.

Each local area enables each resident to be heard. The ideas of local people are scaled up through interactive democracy and governance software. People have a say in ensuring social and environmental justice. We are happy and creative, because we have time to sleep, make slow food, talk to our neighbours, work in communal gardens, play sport or express ourselves in a range of art forms. We have hope for the future. We do not commute long distances to work. We teleport to communal areas and have technology that is inexpensive. Our desire for recognition and status is supported through being rewarded for innovation that supports/*feeds forward* to the next generation. We live not only for ourselves but for our neighbours and the environment that includes us all. We understand and remember what the first nations have taught us that we are of the land and we are of the earth to which we return.

B – Small Adjustments

People make slow annual progress towards goals, which they meet for the benefit of their children and grandchildren.

But they do not move quite fast enough. Young people and those who are able to 'join up dots' help to motivate movement towards a better future.

C – Worst Case: Business as Usual and a Large Carbon Footprint

We continue to believe in economic arguments that ignore the social and environmental dimension. We continue to think that our way of life is sustainable and are not prepared to manage the risks of environmental change by changing our way of life.

We blame the increasing risk of drought, bush fires and floods on 'one off' unrelated events or deny that environmental change can mean rising temperatures in some areas and plummeting temperatures in others as melting ice effects the ocean currents. The sea is used as a dumping ground and it no longer helps to balance our climate.

More and more of us suffer from viruses and food poisoning. Animals are diseased. Most of our rivers are polluted and many have dried up.

We seed the clouds, hoping that 'hubris' will win through. Some people who can afford to *make rain* have water, but others die.

We fight over the last of energy and natural resources.

We export our waste material to poorer nations who 'offer' to store it.

Our government and economy are blamed for the problems, but we do not make any changes, because the market self-regulates.

We are proud to wear designer labels, in designer packages.

We engage in fund raising activities and give money to charity. These small gestures are to enable us to pretend that we are making a difference.

We refuse to an agreement in Copenhagen, because it is bad for the state of the economy.

We are responsible for boundaries; we are they – (Haraway, 1991)

Few thinkers are keen to find ways of conversing across conceptual and spatial boundaries. The implications for ethics, human knowledge and human organisation are vital for this generation and the next.

Alan is one of the thinkers who *is* inclusive.

He understands that we co-shape one another's thinking, just as we are co-shaped by the landscape.

Communication is the basis of ecosystems from the inorganic to organic life and through communication we evolve.

We can move away from zero sum to group togetherness based on planetary consciousness.[4] Now it is up to us.

Dr Janet McIntyre
Associate Professor
Flinders Institute of Public Policy and Management
Flinders University
Adelaide
Australia

Acknowledgements

There are a great many people who have come alongside, encouraged, informed, sustained and influenced me as I have developed my current understandings of natural inclusionality, which are nonetheless inescapably rooted in the idiosyncrasy of my personal observations, studies and interpretations of natural flow form. I hope these companions will find some benefit of their influence sprinkled at least implicitly through the pages of this book. There are some, however, who I feel the need to mention explicitly. First and foremost, my wife, Marion, and daughters, Hazel and Pippa, have witnessed and endured the difficulties and joys that I have experienced as I have worked my passage from objective science to inclusional flow. Lere Shakunle and Ted Lumley helped me early on to make the transition from thinking about 'dynamic boundaries', as described in my book, 'Degrees of Freedom', to recognizing the vital role of 'receptive space' in natural fluidity. Lere's remarkable and original work on 'transfigural mathematics', especially, helped me to recognize the inseparable relationship between 'figural' and 'transfigural' presences in fluid boundaries and 'local-in-nonlocal self-identity'. Jack Whitehead also came alongside early and has been a continual source of support and encouragement in helping me to recognize and describe the educational implications of natural inclusion. Rather more recently, Roy Reynolds has added his deep theological and psychological knowledge and insights, helping me to appreciate and draw out the soul-full dimension of my own and others' creative and empathic lives.

Endnotes

1   At the heart of inclusionality is a natural logic and geometry
    – based on similar perceptions to the 'transfigural mathe-
    matical logic and geometry discovered and elaborated by my
    friend Lere Shakunle – in which all form is understood as
    flow-form, an energetic configuration of space in figure and
    figure in space. And the simple truth underlying this logic
    and geometry is that *space does not stop at boundaries*.
    Correspondingly, we can recognize the following four kinds
    of natural occurrence, as melted versions of the frozen and
    atomized fields and particles of objective science.

POOL – the all-inclusive realm of limitless cosmos, comprising
    both the Infinite Depth of 'space' and the energetic configu-
    rations of its inhabitant flow-forms.

MASSY FLOW-FORMS – of which the most viscous ('solid') get
    treated as discrete particles in rationalistic thinking, which
    also considers even liquid and gaseous phases to consist
    of gatherings of these particles surrounded by space.

SPACE - the unmovable, irremovable Infinite Depth and
    Openness that would be formless and motionless without its
    inhabitant flow-forms.

MASSLESS FLOW-FORMS – with distinctive flow lengths in the
    electromagnetic spectrum, which are perceived conven-
    tionally as sources of 'free energy'.

2   Throughout this essay I use 'we' and 'us' as collective terms
    for the common 'humanity' and 'natural neighbourhood' of
    which I feel 'myself' to be a dynamic inclusion, even though
    the attitudes and behaviour I describe need not apply to all
    in general or anyone in particular. Often these terms may be
    read as 'shorthand' for 'many of us'.

3   von Foerster – socio-cybernetics

4   Earth politics' is the term coined by Beck (1999, 2005) and it

is to this concept that I wish to turn. How can we shift from user-centric narrow pragmatism to user-centric expanded pragmatism, based on choices informed by an understanding of systemic resonance? Multidimensional and multi-spatial design is what is needed for a just and sustainable world. We need to be able to do dialogue for policy and practice in such a way that we take into account time (past, present and future) and place (our own, our neighbours and that of children and their children's) (See McIntyre-Mills 2006 a, c).The nation state is responsible for its citizens, but who is responsible for ensuring the fabric of life is maintained? Nation states need to be aware that zero sum logic is flawed. If people can develop the capacity to think through scenarios it will facilitate pragmatic co-creativity rather than merely imposing decisions based on environmental colonialism resulting from powerful and privileged international positions. People who are struggling to survive have different views. This needs to be appreciated.

References

Briggs, D & Walters, SM (1984) *Plant Variation and Evolution*. 2nd ed. Cambridge University Press

Claxton, G (2006) *The Wayward Mind*. London: Abacus

Curtis, R. (2007) *The Trap – Whatever Happened to Our Dream of Freedom?* BBC TV

Dawkins, R (1989) *The Selfish Gene*. New edition. Oxford University Press

Dowson, CG, Rayner, ADM and Boddy, L (1986) Outgrowth patterns of mycelial cord-forming basidiomycetes from and between woody resource units in soil. *J. Gen. Microbiol.* 132, 203-211

Futuyma, DJ (1986) *Evolutionary Biology*, 2nd Ed. Sunderland, Massachusetts: Sinauer Associates

Goodwin, B (1994) *How the Leopard Changed Its Spots: The Evolution of Complexity*. London: Weidenfeld & Nicolson

Ilyenkov, E (1977) Dialectical Logic. Moscow; Progress Publishers

Keegan, J (2004) The Face of Battle. London: Pimlico

Mandelbrot, B (1977). *The Fractal Geometry of Nature*. New York: Freeman.

Marcuse, H (1964) One-Dimensional Man, London; Routledge and Kegan Paul.

Poincaré, H (1905) *Science and Hypothesis*. Dover Publications, Walter Scott Publishing Company Ltd

Popper, K (1963) Conjectures and Refutations, Oxford, Oxford University Press

Rayner, ADM (1997) *Degrees of Freedom – Living in Dynamic Boundaries*. Imperial College Press, London

Rayner, ADM (2000) Challenging environmental uncertainty: dynamic boundaries beyond the selfish gene. In *Towards an Environment Research Agenda volume 1* (A Warhurst, ed), pp. 215-236. London: Macmillan

Rayner, ADM (2003) Inclusionality – an immersive philosophy of environmental relationships. In *Towards an Environment Research Agenda – a second collection of papers* (A Winnett and A Warhurst, eds.), pp. 5-20. London: Palgrave Macmillan

Rayner, ADM (2004) Inclusionality and the Role of Place, Space and Dynamic Boundaries in Evolutionary Processes. Philosophica, 73, 51-70

Rayner ADM (2006) Natural Inclusion: How to Evolve Good Neighbourhood. Available from http://www.inclusional-research.org/naturalinclusion.php

Rayner, ADM (2008) Natural inclusion – from adversity with love. In *Gifts, Talents and Education*, by B Hymer, J Whitehead and M Huxtable, pp 5-9, Wiley-Blackwell

Shakunle, LO & Rayner, ADM (2008) Superchannel – Inside and beyond superstring: the natural inclusion of one in all – III. *Transfigural Mathematics* **1** (3), 9-55, 59-69

Shakunle, LO and Rayner, ADM (2009) Transfigural foundations for a new physics of natural diversity – the variable inclusion of gravitational space in electromagnetic flow-form. Journal of Transfigural Mathematics, 1 (2), 109-122

Taylor, S (2005) *The Fall*. Winchester, UK, New York, USA: O Books

Wilson, EO (1998) *Consilience – The Unity of Knowledge*. London: Little, Brown and Company

BOOKS

O is a symbol of the world, of oneness and unity. In different cultures it also means the "eye," symbolizing knowledge and insight. We aim to publish books that are accessible, constructive and that challenge accepted opinion, both that of academia and the "moral majority."

Our books are available in all good English language bookstores worldwide. If you don't see the book on the shelves ask the bookstore to order it for you, quoting the ISBN number and title. Alternatively you can order online (all major online retail sites carry our titles) or contact the distributor in the relevant country, listed on the copyright page.

See our website **www.o-books.net** for a full list of over 500 titles, growing by 100 a year.

And tune in to myspiritradio.com for our book review radio show, hosted by June-Elleni Laine, where you can listen to the authors discussing their books.

mySpiritRadio